THE STEEPLE'S SHADOW

On the Myths and Realities of Secularization

David Lyon

WILLIAM B. EERDMANS PUBLISHING COMPANY
GRAND RAPIDS, MICHIGAN

This book was first published in the United Kingdom in conjunction with
Third Way, an evangelical monthly magazine that seeks to provide a
biblical perspective on politics, social ethics, and cultural affairs. Further
information may be obtained from *Third Way*, 37 Elm Road, New Mal-
den, Surrey KT3 3HB, England.

For Jon and Jen
'friends love at all times'

Contents

Preface and Acknowledgements

As a student of 'A' level sociology, in the 1960s, I picked up *The Penguin Survey of the Social Sciences (1965)*, which contained an attack on secularization ideas by David Martin of the London School of Economics and Political Science. That was my first taste of this controversy. Little did I know at the time what significance this would have for my later reflections. As an undergraduate, I was deeply influenced by the movement of cultural criticism and involvement which originated with Francis Schaeffer and Hans Rookmaaker. They were concerned with what happens to Christianity in a 'secular' context. While I benefited tremendously from *'L'Abri'* thinking, I was also uneasy with some accounts of secularization which emerged from this stable.

As a graduate student, I concentrated on the question of beliefs and society in the late Victorian era. This period seemed important both for the so-called 'loss of faith', *and* for religious vitality. But I remained far from satisfied both with the notion of secularization, and with my grasp of it.

Since that time, society has changed. Memories of Christendom are even more faded in Europe, and the cultural landscape of the 1980s bears distinct and permanent traces of the upheavals of the 1960s. New religious movements, and the rise of dogmatic political persuasions on both sides of the Atlantic, pose new questions for 'secularization' theory. The sociology of secularization has been augmented by some penetrating new historical and cultural studies which indicate far more nuance and ambiguity than was once admitted in this area. I have returned periodically to the secularization puzzle, and this book is a result of an ongoing quest.

Although it may appear that this book has gestated for nearly two decades, in fact there was more than one phantom pregnancy along the way. But even by elephants' standards — they take three years to come to birth — progress has been slow. Readers may take comfort from the fact that at least this product is relatively slim. Moreover, the contributions of recent advances in secularization studies have made the text very different from what it once might have been. Another potential problem with elephants is their reputation for clumsiness, and social science jargon often renders books similarly gauche. So I have endeavoured to avoid unnecessary sociologese, and to explain it clearly when a technical term has to be used.

So I hope that the book will be accessible to the general reader, as well as to students of sociology, history and religious studies. It certainly covers topics which should be of interest, not to say concern, to anyone living in late twentieth-century society. For those wanting a more academic treatment, I have presented the main discussion in somewhat more formal dress in 'Rethinking Secularization: Retrospect and Prospect' (*Review of Religious Research,* March 1985). A survey of the literature apears in *Themelios,* September 1984, as 'Secularization: the Fate of Faith in the Modern World?'.

Thanks to David Bebbington, Tim Dean, Os Guinness, Julia Kilbride, George Marsden, David Martin, Derek Tidball and Robert Wuthnow and the publishers who carefully read previous drafts, offering both helpful criticism and timely encouragement. But no blame is due to them for either my errors or my bad judgements. I am indebted to several cohorts of students who were subjected to earlier versions of this material, and who forced me to rethink, at Bradford and Ilkley College, West Yorkshire, Wilfrid Laurier University, Ontario, and at Calvin College, Michigan. Jon and Jen Dening, on whose word-processor this text first appeared, also deserve my gratitude. The dedication to them acknowledges more than this kind service, however.

The last stages of preparation came at a difficult time, when I learned through the protracted hospitalization of my wife, Sue, more of the daily realities of her share in caring for Tim, Abi, Josh and Miriam than I could have learned in any other way. So I am now even more thankful for her patience with my preoccupations. Her support, and the children's, is holding out.

March 1985   *David Lyon*

Introduction

Over the past two hundred years, the steeple's shadow has shrunk drastically. The social influence of organized Christianity has waned. Once a respected and central pillar of society, the Church has been demoted from prominence, and relegated to the social fringes. Frequently the steeple casts no shadow at all, itself overshadowed by the symbolic structures dominating modern cities: the soaring skyscrapers from which commerce, manufacturing, communications, policing and government are administered.

People have learned to look to other sources of insight and knowledge than 'revelation' in order to give meaning and direction to life. No longer under the sheltering steeple, hope is sought in the human capacity to cope. Forecasting, planning and managing, rather than prayer, reliance on God and diligent stewardship are the hallmarks of the secular society. Cost/benefit analysis, getting a market share, efficiency and self-interest are valued more than the love of neighbour or care of creation. Life itself may be 'created' in a test-tube, and 'artificial intelligence' produced microelectronically. No wonder God is rendered redundant.

Key questions about the future of religion in modern society are raised by the ongoing debate over secularization. Will the steeple's shadow continue to contract as science sheds further light and as the power of Christendom is replaced by the secular state? Is the social and cultural influence of the churches in irreversible decline? Will religion itself disappear with the development of hi-tech society? All these issues and more confront us in the term 'secularization'.

The word 'secularization' — or at least the word 'secular' — still dominates our understanding of the religious condition of modern society. With good reason. We cannot grasp what it means to be modern, to be part of an advanced society, without some knowledge of secularization. Of course, I do not necessarily mean *theoretical* knowledge. We all know what is meant when, for instance, people object that a religious professional should not lead a 'secular' movement like the Campaign for Nuclear Disarmament (as does Bruce

1

Kent in Britain). Their meaning is similarly clear when people complain that 'secular' public broadcasting companies should not carry religious programmes, or that prayers should not be said in state-run schools. Everyday life operates happily with the taken-for-granted meanings of 'secular'.

'Secularization' sums up a strikingly significant aspect of modern life. Unlike previous times, and unlike many non-advanced societies, the warp and woof of social life contains little explicit reference to religion (at least as conventionally defined), and is held together only by rational contract and bureaucratic rules. Christianity, which was in several important respects the midwife of modernity, is forsaken or simply forgotten. The cultural capital it once provided has been squandered and allowed to dwindle into insignificance.

The Church as a social institution has been enfeebled by this process. Relegated to the periphery of 'real life', its members all too often accept their situation as defined by society. Over time it is accepted, more or less reluctantly, that the Church has only a very narrow sphere of activity, and that we inhabit a world where folk generally have no time for religion. Church is a kind of relic from yesteryear, maintaining itself by bingo drives and scout-troops, or by adopting new technologies of TV and video in order to attract interest via leisure-time entertainment. The actual claims and demands of the Church's founder, Jesus Christ, have fallen on hard times. The loss of the Church's social position has resulted in a loss of nerve among today's Christians.

These are the realities of secularization, albeit somewhat simplified. But in the hands of some (theologians as much as social scientists!), secularization has had further connotations. The term itself, in its modern usage, grew partly in the soil of misunderstandings of society and history, fertilized above all by the eighteenth-century French Enlightenment. So, for some, it describes a *policy,* something that should be done, rather than just a state of affairs or a social process. For others, it supports popular social beliefs about godlessness, or the disappearance of God, in the modern world.

Some nineteenth-century pundits confidently predicted that the death of religion would be the natural consequence of secularization. Karl Marx said that the need people feel for religion would disappear as the social conditions provoking

2

the need were overcome, and capitalism dismantled. Anthropologists, following the lead of Edward Tylor, pressed evolutionary theory into service in order to show that religion, as a sort of redundant social organ, could become extinct. It was doomed like the Dodo. Sociologists in the line of Max Weber may have been less hostile towards religion, but still held out little prospect for its future. According to Weber, Western society was constructing a self-incarcerating 'iron cage' of a cool, calculating and rational approach to all human affairs. This simply diminishes the realm of the spirit until it is squeezed out altogether.

The assumptions which underlay turn-of-the-century social science have persisted into the present. In modified form, one still encounters both 'evolutionary' accounts of secularization, and also the view that religion cannot survive in a 'rationalized' society. Taken together, these ideas can still give the impression that what Weber called the 'polar night of icy hardness and darkness' is indeed enveloping us. Talk is of a return to the 'dark ages'. The acme of rational calculation would appear to have been reached in the mushrooming computer culture, which reaches not only into the public world of commerce and manufacture, but also the private domestic sphere. Those computer terminals certainly do pose further problems with which Christianity has to come to terms. But the misleading side is the impression given that, because of rationalization, modern society simply has no room for any religion.

This is one of the myths of secularization. A myth is a story which is partially true, but which also obscures the truth by exaggerating one aspect of it, or just through popular, oversimplified elaboration. Those (mercifully fewer today) who hold to a 'strong' version of secularization see it as an irresistible social force, moving steadily forward wherever modernity has found a foothold, and having more-or-less the same effects in all contexts. They are prone to minimize evidence of Christian vitality as a mere evolutionary freak, and to miss altogether other possible dimensions of life which have evaded 'rationalization' or the encroachments of the secular state. This includes both the 'new religious movements'—from the Charismatic revival within the churches to the Moonies or Divine Light Mission beyond them—and also

3

the persistence of ritual or the emergence of novel 'sacred domains' in the modern world.

Other myths of secularization include these ideas: That Christianity's most important task is the supposed social function of providing some cohesion or sense of togetherness within a given society; that there was once a 'golden age' of faith, from which Western society has declined; that secularization happens automatically wherever 'modernity' has arrived, without help from those who wish to speed it up and without regard to others who may try to resist it. Each of these myths has been criticized before, but not, so far as I know, in one place.

This book is a state-of-the-art survey of secularization studies. It breaks no new ground in unearthing fresh evidence or proposing a novel theory (although I do bring in some of my own research, and also suggest possible directions for future inquiry). What it does is to draw together the diverse threads of secularization studies in order to highlight their strong and to expose their weak points.

Needless to say, this is not a detached, 'neutral' task, although I do make every attempt to be accurate and fair. The guiding perspective derives from biblical themes and insights, by which I try to make sense of often conflicting accounts. This approach, dubbed 'critical integration' (in *Sociology and the Human Image*) makes explicit the role of one's commitments in choosing between theories, while at the same time allowing social science to scrutinize those commitments. This wider perspective actually helps defuse some disagreements between secularization theorists, while at the same time opening up fruitful lines of investigation.

'Secularization' has gone through phases of favour and disfavour. Mid-twentieth century sociologists built up the story using raw materials provided by the classical theorists. Theologians picked up the term, and used it enthusiastically (but fairly uncritically) in the 1960s, actually to proclaim human autonomy as an authentic result of biblical faith. Cutting right across this came David Martin's celebrated critique, which successfully initiated serious debate over the definitions and meaning of the term. Historians, keen to demonstrate their openness to social science in the 1970s, produced several of their own specific studies of 'secularization', which was grist to the same mill. They were also in a good position to temper the confidence of some sociologists in the reliability or universal applicability of 'secularization'. In fact, several sociologists took a leaf from their book. By the early 1980s, 'cultural analysis' was being revived and revamped as a serious discipline. This takes seriously all evidence of so-called 'non-rational' as well as highly rational aspects of modern society, from punk and pornography to management and microchips. Current relations between 'Church and world' also fit under this rubric. The result is greater concern with what is actually occurring in 'secular' society.

Also in the 1980s, especially in the USA, 'secularization' is receiving heavy criticism. As it happens, some Americans have always been suspicious of the term, thinking (with some justification) it had more to do with the European than the 'New World' experience. But today the danger is that the critique will get out of hand. Despite the prevalent and misleading myths surrounding 'secularization', it would be foolish to try to dispense with the term altogether. As I said at the outset, 'secularization' still sums up a strikingly significant aspect of modern life. The myths must be debunked (and we review various debunking efforts here), but we must not lose sight of the kernel of fundamental social insight lurking behind the halo of myth. It is as indispensible for understanding North American (or Australasian) as it is for European culture.

In a sense, we move beyond an exclusive concern with *secularization* studies, in an attempt to recover what was in fact the vision of early social scientists: the ambition to throw light on the complex pattern of relationships between religion and society. This not only means that secularization is taken very seriously, but that criticisms of it for distorting and obscuring social and religious reality are taken equally seriously. 'Secularization' is only a concept. But we use concepts to organize what we know about, and thus how we participate in, the world. If they distract us from seeing what is actually happening, we are in danger of myopia or blindness. Whether we are thus handicapped, or better enabled to *act* in an informed way in today's society, depends—at least in part—on the sharpness of our conceptual vision.

1: Measuring the Steeple's Shadow

After a brief look at what is usually meant by 'secularization', this chapter tackles two problems which must be faced by anyone trying to understand the relationship between religion and modern society. These problems are, firstly, what is 'religion' anyway? and, secondly, how do we understand the process of history to take place?

Does the fact that the 'steeple' casts its shadow over less and less of today's society mean that modern people are 'less religious', or that the Church has lost its grip, or what? Such questions cannot be answered unless we are clear about what we mean by 'religion'. Likewise with the historical problem. Any word ending in '-ization' must refer to something which happens over time, an historical process. Is secularization, to put it crudely, something which just happens to us, or something we can accelerate or retard, or both?

Readers wishing to move more quickly to the details of social life in a secular world may want to skip this chapter, and the next, for the time being, and start their reading with 'the secularization story' (chapter 3). However, the foundation laid in this chapter, and the background to secularization theories (and theorists) which appears in the next, do enter the argument later on. Answers to this chapter's questions both show how important it is to understand secularization, and also help us criticize its associated myths.

Many variations on the theme exist, but a commonly accepted story of secularization runs something like this. Once upon a time religion was at the centre of life. Before the world was modernized people ordered their lives around certain beliefs and rituals associated with supernatural beings. In the medieval period, this religious order of life was clearly visible: from the blessings sought for birth, marriage and death to the divine right of kings.

Folk found all they needed for the explanation (and perhaps healing) of illness and accident, in religion. The same source yielded an account of the cosmos in which everything had its

6

proper place, the so-called 'great chain of being' (Lovejoy, 1960). Religion not only told us who we were, but also what we should believe and how we should live. It gave a framework, and clearly-defined boundaries. It even formed the base of early education and welfare institutions. The priest, joined later by the doctor and lawyer, was regarded as a guardian of what was most important in society. Then something happened. Whether gradually or suddenly, the shadows of hope and fear thrown by the symbolic steeple at the centre of the village began to recede. As industrialization transformed the face of Europe, so organized religion became one of the casualties. People uprooted from their traditional habitat were exposed to new influences on lifestyle and belief. The Church, demoted from its privileged position near the social apex, lost control of spheres of influence, such as education, once thought of as its natural province. Simultaneously, modern science burgeoned, posing perceived threats to supernaturalist ways of thinking. A cool, calculating approach crept cancerously into all areas of life, seen above all in the profit-and-efficiency drive of capitalism.

To study secularization, we must examine and describe the contracting shadow cast by Church on society. The waning influence of church religion over public and even, to an extent, private life is what secularization is all about. This is the view subjected to scrutiny here. It is not plain wrong. Rather, it oversimplifies and thus distorts our view.

Getting to grips with what happened to religion and society as the 'forces' of modernization spread through the 'Old World' of Europe and the 'New World' of North America is of vital importance. It cannot be done without grappling with 'secularization'. But 'secularization' does not exist in a philosophical vacuum. It is embedded in forms of interpretation. So before proceeding further, I must come clean about the kind of interpretation adopted here.

Two questions are crucial. One, 'secularization of what?'. In other words, we must examine what is meant by 'religion'. Much hangs on this. Do we accept Parson Thwackum's definition, so nicely portrayed for us by Henry Fielding: 'When I mention religion I mean the Christian religion; and not only the Christian religion, but the Protestant religion; and not only the Protestant religion, but the Church of England' (quoted in Marty, 1982, p. 155)? Or might we be willing to entertain a broader notion of religion?

Two, as we are discussing secular*ization,* we clearly refer to an historical process. So the question of history cannot be avoided. Is it just something that happens to us, or do we 'make history', or both? And once it has happened, is there any sense in which we may return to recover what has been lost? Or are we then doomed to walk the road thus begun? What is our time-scale? Should we consider what has happened since the Industrial Revolution as somehow more significant than what went before?

Old Wives' Tales: the Problem of Religion

For most people in the West, the word 'religion' conjures up a picture of a meeting, usually presided over by a man in a special uniform, in which phrases about a non-human being are repeated in music, read from a book, or elaborated by the leader of the meeting. Even if this kind of assembly has not been experienced directly, some knowledge of it is readily available in Sunday TV slots. This is, of course, the religion of the churches, the traditional, conventional, official religion of Christendom.

Massive variation occurs even within religion understood thus. Religious buildings may for instance feature the breathtaking grandeur of a French cathedral, the overtly theological message of a Scottish crown-shaped tower, the hi-tech hype of a Crystal Cathedral, or the austere simplicity of a Christian Brethren chapel. Again, what happens inside the buildings varies enormously, from solemn silence and quiet ritual to noisy exuberance and total participation. Nevertheless, what these diverse patterns have in common is the institutional expression of Christianity: church religion.

But is the boundary of religion to be found at the church door? Is everything outside the pale non-religious? For that matter, is everything going on within the institutional Church equally religious? In Victoria's England or Reagan's America church attendance may have as much to do with respectability as religiosity. And what of the high proportion of families who converge on a religious building for birth-ceremony, marriage or funeral, but who otherwise do not darken its doors? Their passage through life may be made more meaningful or legitimate by this use of this religious agency, but most clergy would take a dim view of 'three-times-per-lifetime' attendance in all parishioners!

Or take a festival like Christmas. An assortment of rituals is bundled together here. As Robert Bocock says, 'It is a key festival of the Christian religious year; a family ritual; a ritual of gift-exchange; a ritual of Mammon; and a ritual of the winter solstice' (Bocock, 1974, p. 114). The Christian aspect is essential, yet for most people it has no deeper significance than the children's nativity play and the pictures on the cards. The gift-exchange ritual, though commercially exploited, also exists independently of advertising. Likewise the cards, the giving and receiving of which carry such tremendous emotional freight.

Christmas revolves round a dinner, to which grandparents are duly invited. In Bocock's words, 'The family is ritually unified over three generations by the eating of this meal' (Bocock, 1974, p. 115). Christmas in fact furnishes us with a fine example of what is often called 'common religion'. That is, the religion of the common people. It is residually Christian but persists well beyond the reach of any Christian institution. The family is also centrally involved.

Mention of the family brings up another dimension of 'religion'. Reflect for a moment on the possible ambiguity of the phrase 'family worship'. Emphasize *worship*, and we are in the realm of those who still take seriously Old Testament injunctions to teach the next generation the essence of true religion. But put the accent on *family*, and we enter, as they say, a different ball-game. Worship *of* the family is placed by some alongside sexuality, self-expression and autonomy as modern forms of religious devotion. Needless to say, 'ball-games' themselves may also be found in this category. It is argued that, analogously to belief in a Creator or participation in the Eucharist, ball-games may bestow symbolic meaning on life.

The debate over such widely differing definitions of religion has been long and fierce. Pioneer sociologist Max Weber, who contributed much to secularization studies, himself avoided tackling the definitional issue head on. He bequeathed to later generations only an implicit definition which seemed, unflatteringly, to place religion in a non-rational realm. Not only does the debate over existing definitions continue today, new ones are also being added to the list (see for example the 'materialist' definition in Turner, 1983).

Three definitions of religion are hiding in the above discussion. One refers to the religion of the churches as the real thing. So when in Christendom churches were a more 'natural' part of social life, one could perhaps talk of 'Christian society'. Loss of the social prominence of the churches would then be 'secularization' as 'decline of religion'. In this case, the organization defines the scope of 'religion'.

A second definition is 'common' or 'folk' religion (Towler, 1974, pp. 145–62). Enter the 'old wives' tales'. This area of experience may include residual reference to church religion but, as with Christmas, is not limited by it. A crucifix may be worn for luck, and a christening be done as a sort of holy insurance. A whole set of beliefs may be woven together in a manner coherent to those who share it, punctuated by Christian motifs but in other ways alien to conventional religion. Secularization, as the loss of social prominence of the churches, may slide right over the surface of these 'subterranean theologies' (as David Martin calls them). This means we should stop short of saying that secularization obliterates the religious life as such.

The third definition still sees religion as giving meaning to life, but does not require any conventional religious baggage of creed or custom. Religion is here seen in everyday life themes, such as the family, football, or the more abstract commitment to 'bettering oneself'. Symbols and ritual are still of the essence, but no reference at all need be made to God or the supernatural. So this is 'natural' (or 'implicit' or 'invisible') religion (Luckmann, 1967). But how does one choose between different definitions?

Definition one, 'official' or 'conventional' religion, has sociological merit. This has the advantage of clarity about what is included and excluded, so genuine similarities and differences may be emphasized. As Alan Gilbert says, 'There are obvious grounds for dissatisfaction with a definition which fails to make a distinction in kind between a football fan's devotion to his team, however total and impassioned it may be, and a devout Christian's reverence for a transcendent God' (Gilbert, 1980, p. 5). Any systematic social historical analysis which depends on being able to discriminate between religious and other factors in order to comment on cause-and-effect relationships requires a fairly tight definition of the phenomena under investigation (Robertson, 1970, p. 43).

The best known secularization writers use this conventional definition of religion. While he thinks of religion as something that 'transcends the traditional churches', Bryan Wilson says it must nevertheless pertain 'only to those activities that make some explicit reference to a supernatural source of values' (Wilson, 1976, p. 4). David Martin agrees that in order to say anything intelligent about secularization this kind of definition is necessary. But he stresses the costs: *religious structure* becomes the focus, even though 'religion is a creature of the realm of symbol, feeling, and meaning' (Martin, 1978, p. 13). Gilbert is right, then, to say that 'it is in the interactions between the "church" and the "world" that the historian of secularization finds his central theme' (Gilbert, 1980, p. xiii).

But what of the other definitions? David Martin is clearly reluctant to put all his analytical eggs in one basket. He once described the British as pursuing a 'deistic religion-in-general which combines fairly high practice of personal prayer with a considerable degree of superstition' (Martin, 1973, p. 86, see also David Clark's study of the Yorkshire fishing village, Staithes, 1982). Hardly a tight, conventional definition! In the USA, Robert Bellah observes a similarly vague 'religion'. Widespread agreement is found among those who differ on other matters, that God exists, that he rewards virtue and punishes vice, and so on. This phenomenon is outside conventional churches, and is often associated with events of national significance, such as presidential inaugurations. Bellah calls it 'civil religion' (Bellah, 1970). It is obviously compatible with 'common' religion.

While not enjoying church support, such religious manifestations are not random or individually based. They are passed on from one generation to the next in ways which can be charted. Apparently innocent childhood games may be one context in which common religion is passed through peer groups. They may even outlive some sects or denominations, as the example of Christmas shows. Being outside the churches also means that such religion suffers less from secularization (as the pulling apart of Church and world).

Those who hanker after precise measurement and neat explanation in social science are least happy with the notion

11

of 'natural' religion (even more so if it goes under the elusive heading of 'invisible' religion!). Computing the length of the steeple's shadow is difficult enough. Trying to say something which will pass sociological muster about belief in the family, or in science itself, is even harder. Yet this is exactly the problem that faces anthropologists struggling to understand rites and symbols alien to them. Which is why a more anthropological perspective is helpful at this point.

Clifford Geertz sees religion in terms of symbols. Such symbols motivate people and establish their mindsets by giving a general sense of the order of existence. This 'sense' of order appears to correspond with what really is (Geertz, 1966, p. 2). Without doubt, this definition is broader than 'official' or 'common' religion. It need not deal with the supernatural, or even with the 'ultimate' (contrast Yinger, 1970, p. 7). So sociological (not to mention historical) merit *also* resides with this definition. Rather than attempt to contain all kinds of expressed or discernible belief or ritual practice within the conventional ambit of church religion, why not admit to a sacred realm beyond the lich-gate? It would indeed be strange, after signs of the sacred having permeated all known societies in world history up till now, that suddenly we enter a 'post-religious' age.

Another advantage of this definition is that it puts religion in close contact with the rest of life. It is not a separate compartment. Rathei it is part of our general cultural equipment for making sense of the world, and refers directly to the business of everyday life. This applies as much to the 'spirits of the mountains' believed in by Ecuadorian Indians (for whom mountains form the physical context of life) as to the twentieth-century suburbanite who 'believes in' the family. Are some people sceptical that 'familism occupies an important place in the sacred cosmos of modern industrial societies' (Luckmann, 1967, p. 112)? Then why does their scepticism not extend to Latin America, where, as many accept, mountains are sacred symbols?

The usual response to the difficulty of competing definitions of religion is to plump for one or the other, and to work within that frame. The danger of this solution, if each definition does have its own merits, is that important dimensions of religious and cultural life will be missed. So why insist that the definitions are mutually exclusive? Church historians and sociologists of religion have sometimes been guilty of ironic oversight. By studying the institutional fortunes of Christianity they have given the impression, like Parson Thwackum, that Christianity admits to the existence of none but formal religions.

Yet the apostle Paul, no less than Jesus himself, apparently had little trouble convincing the early Christians that religion could have a divine or natural focus. Paul spells this out in the first chapter of the Letter to the Romans, where he distinguishes between the worship and service of 'created things rather than the Creator'. Your heart is where your treasure is, said Jesus.

From this point of view, then, holding more than one definition of religion makes good sense. As far as our main theme is concerned, this perspective does not allow secularization to mean the decline of religion as such. This need not obscure real and apparent slimming-down of church adherence, or act as a palliative to those anxious about a contracting Christian influence on society. Rather, being clear about what kind of religion we are discussing enables us to be more accurate about secularization.

Secularization studies rightly document the splitting away of the Church from other social institutions. Such studies are also quite correct in noting modern society's apparent unconcern with explicitly transcendent matters and supernatural explanation. Secularization may be thought of as the lowering of eyes to the temporal horizon. But at the same time secularization studies cannot ignore the thick and resilient undergrowth of common religion, which has outlived the atrophy of the churches' public impact. (Even a thoroughgoing secularization theorist like Wilson concedes that 'nonlogical elements' continue unabated in modern society! (Wilson, 1973, p. 504)). Similarly, it is misleading to say that secularization somehow severs our sense of symbols as a means of finding order and meaning for life. Understanding today's sacred symbols is arguably as important as documenting the local eclipse of Christian religious symbols.

Jettisoning exclusive definitions of religion brings us closer to the real world in a further way. The neat and tidy world of the scientist may be disturbed by holding to more than one definition at once. But perhaps to acknowledge that there is more to religion than meets the ecclesiastical eye better reflects what is happening in society today. It does also make for paradox. If the apostle is correct, then secular symbols (those associated with the temporal, passing world) may attract religious devotion!

Of course, readers might well object that allowing for more than one definition of religion by appeal to biblical sources is a sociologically suspect procedure. After all, did not Peter Berger recommend that sociologists of religion follow the principle of 'methodological atheism'? By this, he meant that personal beliefs about the ultimate validity of a given religion should be 'bracketed' during sociological investigation. While this stance helps avoid the partisanship of *sociologie religieuse,* which simply turns sociology into the fact-finding handmaiden of the Church, it also has problems.

Though a superficially attractive idea, some have been worried about 'methodological atheism's' apparent association with atheism as such (despite Berger's distancing himself from that). Others fear that, following this way, no-one's religious beliefs can be taken seriously; the observer's working assumption will be that they are untrue. (The debate is summarized in Gill, 1975, pp. 31 – 4.) The nub of the matter, however, is whether it is *possible* to insulate sociology from 'non-empirical' factors such as political persuasion or religious commitment.

To be worth doing, sociology must be an empirical discipline, which means that theories should be constrained by observable facts. But they are only *constrained* by those facts, not *determined* by them. A theory which proposes, for instance, that modern conditions militate more strongly against the practice of Christianity than did previous social circumstances, emerges from more than mere detached observation of facts. Non-empirical judgements must be made, not only about the definition and practice of Christianity now, but also about how difficult it was to be a Christian three or four hundred years ago. While sociology should be rigorously accurate, fair, honest and parsimonious, it can never be a *purely* empirical discipline in which theories are built on the solid foundation of observable facts. So I would agree that something like 'methodological theism' (Dekker, 1979) would be just as valid sociologically as methodological atheism (see also Lyon, 1983, 1983b). At base, social theory

14

cannot evade 'pollution' by religious (any more than political) presuppositions.

There is good common sense and sociological reason for accepting that we must work with more than one definition of religion. But this also fits nicely with a pespective derived from biblical sources, which makes it consistent with my own commitment. After all, if there is such a thing as 'true religion', then substitutes for the genuine article are likely to be sought as zealously as the real thing. I would sooner state my position clearly, acknowledging that Christian commitment does affect my analysis, and leave the reader to judge the result.

All too often, history and sociology have treated religion as 'old wives' tales', in the sense that they can be dismissed as less than rational. Religion has also been seen as a dispensable aspect of human life, replaceable in the modern world by advanced forms of cognition. So far from adopting that position here, we argue that religion be taken very seriously, in all its dimensions: conventional, common and natural, as an ongoing, intrinsic aspect of society and culture. Religion should not be written off as 'old wives' tales'. In fact, old wives' tales should be investigated as religion.

Fairy Tales: the Problem of History

All fairy tales begin 'once upon a time'. In history, this opener is out of place. The secularization story, as we have already noted, commences with: 'Once upon a time religion was at the centre of life'. While 'old wives' tales' should perhaps be treated to more academic seriousness than they are sometimes accorded, 'fairy tales' remain suspect (see David Martin, 1969, p. 36).

The issues faced here are of two kinds. One is the nineteenth-century before-and-after-modernization approach, which exaggerates the differences made by industrial capitalism. This view also makes changes sound as if they are irreversible, a view bolstered by adopting an evolutionary outlook. The other issue follows from it, namely that medievalism is the once-upon-a-time (at least in Europe; the USA provides an interesting contrast). The difficulties with this are: firstly, that medievalism, as a coherent society suffused with official religion, probably never existed.

Secondly, that to take this supposed medievalism as a baseline for secularization does less than justice to the development of Christianity.

Firstly, we consider the issue of evolutionary explanation. Secularization theories did not arise in Europe by accident. European societies were first to experience the realities of secularization, insofar as they are associated with the emergence of industrial capitalism. Nor was it coincidence that those secularization theories were frequently flavoured by 'evolution'. For evolution was a leading motif of later nineteenth-century thought and opinion. Intellectuals hailed it as the key to the riddles of the universe, and as such it had universal application. For an age of overwhelming social transformation — from steam-railway mobility to the widening democratic vote — the idea of evolutionary development held the promise of an explanatory catch-all (see Burrow, 1966).

But the one-way street of evolutionary secularization theory is quite inept. The difficulties are more than mere hiccups within a steady trend of, say, declining Christian influence. For instance, during the period of most intense social transformation in industrializing Europe, the 'non-conformist conscience' was a political force to be reckoned with (see Bebbington, 1982). One celebrated example of such pressure on government was the abandonment in 1841 of Sunday Cabinet meetings!

The thrust of this book is frankly anti-evolutionary. The Victorians were mistaken in the effort to apply evolution to society. The result was that they overlooked the *continuities* between the pre-industrial age and their own, and tended to conceive of history in rather mechanical terms. Secularization, as the notion was carried into the twentieth century, was viewed as a kind of juggernaut which rides roughshod over social relationships and religious beliefs. The upshot was that 'massive social forces' came to dominate social science thinking, at the expense of concern with individual and group action.

Let us be quite clear. I am not denying the logic of sociology by appealing to *individual* explanation. I am rather criticizing evolutionary ideas for their effect of making social change too mechanical a process. The patterning of history and the structuring of social relationships does not happen behind people's backs. Human beings actively contribute to the social systems which simultaneously shape their lives. I am convinced that any worthwhile social and cultural analysis must take this view (see Wuthnow, 1984, p. 261). Take an example from secularization studies. We are often urged, and rightly so, to make a distinction between secular*ization* and secular*ism* (see for instance Chadwick, 1975). British Humanist Association members are secular*ists,* who complain and campaign about the one-time privileged position of Christianity in education and the mass media. Secularization, on the other hand, might be the term used to describe how that privileged position is attenuated by the increasing social divergence of church and state. Secularization is about an abstract process. Secularism is about individuals and groups actively combating the power of organized religion. A secularizing society is fertile soil for secularism to flourish in; secularist movements may accelerate the secularization process.

Secularization is not the blind, mechanical process that evolutionists suppose. Of course, certain actions do have unintended consequences. It seems likely, for instance, that English non-conformist political activity sometimes detracted from the chapels' impact on Christian piety. But people also knowingly respond to social situations and try to alter them or conserve them. Such reflection enters the fabric of history and may even divert its patterns. Evolutionism underestimates such human knowledgeability, with the result, as Campbell has said, that sociologists often overlooked the role of irreligious movements as agents of secularization (1971, p. 6). This book takes such knowledgeability seriously, not least in its readers! The notion of knowledgeability also accords with the general point, made by Richard Fenn, that 'secularization proceeds or fails because particular groups and organizations *want* secularization to proceed or fail' (1978, p. 78).

The second main issue to which we must pay attention is the 'age of faith'. Pitirim Sorokin, for example, takes as baseline for his study of secularization 'the religiously animated medieval Christian culture and society' (quoted in Dobbelaere, 1981, p. 31). Since this time, he says, Christian revelation has been demoted, the arts have lost their Christian inspiration, Christian morality has been eroded and the Church has declined in importance as a social institution. At

17

a more popular level, Harry Blamires regrets the demise of a 'Christian mind'. He says a 'religious view of life, one which sets all earthly issues in the context of the eternal,' is no longer available (Blamires, 1963, p. 4). It is one thing to recognize, from a Christian perspective, the spiritual bankruptcy of much modern culture, and the often pathetic collusion of organized Christianity in allowing itself to be shaped by such an outlook. It is another thing to assume that 'once-upon-a-time' the situation was vastly different.

If one begins with such a base-line, one cannot but conclude that traditional religion has fallen on hard times. From the perspective of Bryan Wilson's claim that 'Religious thinking, religious practices and religious institutions were once the very centre of life in Western society', the churches' prospects appear bleak indeed (Wilson, 1969, p. ix).

The age-of-faith idea is not hard to dismantle using the evidence we have today. Gabriel Le Bras, a French Catholic scholar, has criticized the related term, 'dechristianization', on the grounds that historical testimony to a 'Christian' past is poor. Christianity was hardly a matter of conviction in France. As he says, it was 'the religion of the French by virtue of the monarchial constitution' (quoted in Goodridge, 1975, p. 385). Christianity was the 'ruler's religion', not the religion of the masses.

Humbert of Romans (1200—1277) wrote of his Italian experience that 'It must be noted that the poor rarely go to church, rarely to sermons; so that they know little of what pertains to their salvation' (Goodridge, 1975, p. 387). And in England things were little different. According to Keith Thomas, in the Elizabethan period 'a substantial proportion of the population regarded organized religion with an attitude which varied from cold indifference to frank hostility' (Thomas, 1971, pp. 171—2). The cumulative effect of this kind of evidence is to hang a heavy question mark over the notion of an 'age of faith', at least in the sense of a recognizably *Christian* one. (In fact, the very notion of 'medievalism', as a coherent social-cultural system, is now in some doubt.)

Bryan Wilson does qualify his age-of-faith claim by referring to the extent of 'church-control' over society (Wilson, 1976, pp. 7—11). Secularization then becomes almost measurable (Wilson's intention is to make it such) as the contraction of the organized Church's power over time. Others

18

call this 'laicization', the process whereby affairs once under church jurisdiction pass into 'lay' hands. This is fair enough.

But a nagging doubt remains as to the extent of 'church control', at least over the lower social echelons. Was the 'religion of the rulers' ever embraced to any significant extent by the 'ruled'? According to Ladurie (1980, p. 305) 'specifically Christian piety was always the attribute of an élite in the Middle Ages'. So class difference is crucial. Established religion probably did play a part in making the rulers appear legitimate (at least in their own eyes), but was less convincing to the 'ruled'. This does not of course mean that the latter were entirely devoid of religion. Magic, superstition and tradition — albeit peppered with Christian piety — was the more likely diet of the medieval masses.

While Protestants as well as Catholics have subscribed to the medieval age-of-faith idyll, a peculiarly Protestant variant is also available. If the medievalist view is accepted, then the Reformation must be viewed as accelerating secularization. This is exactly what many, following Max Weber, have said. Protestantism, both by fostering a rational and individualist outlook, and by forcing a schism within Christendom, hastened secularization. In Weber's celebrated phrase, Christianity became its own gravedigger.

Such a negative slant on the Reformation is hardly congenial to its descendants! While British Protestants, who are divided over their continuity with pre-Reformation times (Anglicans often stress continuity; non-conformists often reject it), are ambivalent about medievalism, Americans often regard their Puritan settlers' culture as an age-of-faith. Popular evangelical apologetes frequently hark back to America's 'Christian origins'. Francis Schaeffer, for example, assumes that America once flourished as a Christian society, from which contemporary culture has declined (Schaeffer, 1976).

But when exactly did this putative age-of-faith flower? In fact, as George Marsden shows, the legacy of the Puritans and their descendants is deeply contradictory. The political practice of the Puritan settlers blurred precisely the distinction between church and state to which they were in principle committed. Marsden does not for a moment deny the huge and enduring impact of Puritanism on the shaping of American culture. Americans often saw themselves as a 'new

Israel'. But it does not follow that a 'Christian culture' was thus formed. To quote Marsden again, 'probably the principal factor turning the Puritan cultural achievement into a highly ambiguous one was . . . the idea that one can create a truly Christian culture' (Marsden, 1983, p. 219).

The first governor of Massachusetts Bay, John Winthrop, worked out his biblical philosophy of society and politics before ever setting foot on American soil. His admirable intention of applying God's law to every aspect of life foundered on the same rock that bedevils many similar attempts. He had to assume that the entire Massachusetts society was essentially Christian. Marsden says this was due in part to the Europeanism of the Puritans. Their historical experience of a thousand years of living in 'Christendom', a concept not dispelled by classical Puritanism, led them to think of America as a 'new Israel' (1983, p. 222).

At best, this meant that political life was seen to be 'under God'. Few Christians would take exception to that (though too few take care properly to work out its implications for today). At worst, it helped create the climate in which the notorious Salem witchcraft executions took place. Puritans such as the deviant Roger Williams have rarely been accorded the same posthumous respect as their compatriots who left such a paradoxical legacy. Williams actually took seriously the Church—state separation by insisting that the Church is a spiritual entity united in devotion to Christ. As Marsden concludes, 'Despite their strenuous efforts to apply good principles in building a model Christian society that would be a "City on a Hill" for the world to imitate, we are left uncertain that the city in question is the City of God' (1983, p. 224).

By highlighting the paradoxical and ambiguous in these examples, I am not trying to suggest that there is an alternative, *un*ambiguous way of discussing secularization. Rather, my intention is to demonstrate that talk of secularization immediately plunges us into the rhetoric of historical debate, and that the least one can do is to display the basic assumptions with which one begins. My own view, over against those which try to evade ambiguity by means of the simplistic secularization which starts with an age-of-faith, is to accept it as an accurate reflection of the very subject under discussion. Ambiguity and paradox lie near the core of secularization studies.

One major paradox is this. One may take medievalism as baseline in order to examine the process whereby one-time church tasks and authority are transferred to the state. But is this a secularization of *Christianity*? If Roger Williams of Massachusetts Bay was correct, then the notion of church control over society is a fundamental aberration from pristine Christian community. Medievalism, in this view, would be the low point, not the fulfilment of Christianity! As Roger Mehl states, medievalism 'resurrected the synthesis of pagan antiquity between the city and the world of the gods', and thus it lost sight of the Good News (1970, p. 60). Secularization studies of this sort damage the integrity of historic Christianity by definition, if its only salient feature is its political clout.

Let us be clear. Christianity is intended to be applied in all areas of life, all sectors of society. From New Testament times, 'Jesus is Lord' has been the uncompromising manifesto of the faithful, the retreat of some to the ghetto or monastery notwithstanding. So these economic, political or cultural dimensions are not alien invasions of 'spiritual' territory. Responsibility in these and other areas is a vital aspect of the Christian response. But at the same time, Christianity refuses to be exclusively associated with such dimensions; Jesus's kingdom is 'not of this world'. When temporal power ousts spiritual reality, or when society-in-general is confused with the Church, then Christianity itself is diminished. Secularization stories which contribute to such misunderstanding are, from this point of view, irresponsible.

So much for fairy tales. There is no straightforward version of the secularization drama. The simple story is suspect. Ambiguity abounds. Paradox proliferates. History is plain messy. But this fact does not excuse sloppy history writing! Care over detail only leads into greater complexity. The temptation must be resisted to relieve complexity by appeal to the simplisms of 'evolution'. Rethinking our approach to historical material is part of the argument that takes us beyond secularization.

Secularization as Problematic
The reader's patience is poorly rewarded if my tentative conclusion is 'secularization gives us problems'! Wait. The word 'problematic' has a technical sense. In this book I am issuing an invitation to come with me 'beyond' unexamined

21

and taken-for-granted versions of secularization. I would eagerly abandon the term, but am at a loss to find suitable alternatives to it. So it may be retained as a 'problematic'.

A 'problematic' is a 'rudimentary organization of a field of study' (Abrams, 1982, p. xv). It suggests directions along which to look, and holds together in a loose way different things which seem relevant. Karel Dobbelaere calls it a 'sensitizing' concept, for the same reason (1981, p. 10). In its original sense, secularization described the transfer of ecclesiastical property to princely control. Even there, it thus 'sensitizes' us to the questions surrounding Church—state relations. But in and of itself, it explains nothing. Rather, it is the thing to be explained.

In what follows, we examine some of the different dimensions suggested by the secularization problematic. (See Larry Shiner (1967) for a still-useful guide through six possible dimensions.) Although discussion of church, common and natural religion is woven into the arguments, our main focus is on the wider society. We look at the gradual *disengagement,* or 'uncoupling' of Church and society as a central theme. Parallel with this, however, is the idea that society has become increasingly *rationalized,* meaning crudely that people turn more readily to technique than to prayer or providence to cope with or organize life.

But, as we have hinted, secularization cannot mean a simple transfer from 'religious' to 'scientific' thinking. More is involved. So we must also bear in mind other cultural layers where symbols and meaning may not be expressed in traditional religious or scientific terms. In such realms, 'sacralization' may occur as belief is *transposed,* as it were, into a different key. At the same time, what goes on inside the churches cannot be ignored. Their 'inner secularization', 'inner renewal', or plain 'persistence' is another unavoidable aspect of this problematic.

Measuring the steeple's shadow—if this means fact-grubbing—is not really what this book is about. Rather, we are immersed in a fascinating and crucially significant controversy about the role of religion in the modern world. It is a controversy which spills well over the boundaries of the sociology of religion. Contemporary cultural analysis cannot dispense with some reference to 'secularization', any more than general historical sociology can. That—not to mention its decisive impact on Christian practice, which I assume throughout—is why it is important. And in what follows we suggest why the concept of 'secularization' requires radical revision.

2: From Sacred Canopy to Iron Cage

A tree's roots, the secret of how it stands up, lie beneath the surface. The secularization story known to the twentieth century has its roots in the nineteenth; thus to understand it properly we have to dig down to those roots.

In this chapter we return to the early stages of the modern world in order to explore what the massive changes in society meant to nineteenth-century observers. Pioneer social scientists were united in seeing the significance of religion to traditional society, but differed on what would happen as industrial society matured.

Many, delighted with the apparent success of 'evolution' as a way of explaining the history of the natural world, pressed it into service as a key to society and history as well. The results of this strategy become clear in the rest of the book. Another aspect of secularization ideas took its bearings from the European 'Enlightenment', in which 'Reason' was enthroned and 'faith' denigrated. So as we shall see, many studies of 'secularization' have themselves been enthusiastically secular.

We also meet two 'classical' social scientists of religion, Frenchman Emile Durkheim, and German Max Weber. For simplicity's sake we concentrate on one each of their ideas. So we encounter the progressive 'uncoupling' of different segments of society, as industrialization and capitalism develop. In this process, the Church is prised away from its traditional ties with state and society. And we also look at what Weber called 'rationalization', the way in which society becomes increasingly subject to rules, regulations and a scientific outlook. Secularization has a lot to do with both these notions.

The terms 'sacred canopy' and 'iron cage' were not coined simultaneously. They belong to different eras of social thought. But I am deliberately setting them alongside one another to help capture the nineteenth-century feeling that a cultural sea-change was occurring. Many believed that they were 'between two worlds', as Matthew Arnold put it, the one dying, the other waiting to be born. Religion, and its feared loss, was at the heart of this perceived social transformation.

The 'sacred canopy' is Peter Berger's more recent metaphor for religion as an overarching feature of pre-modern societies. Medieval Catholicism yields a fine example in which all life, apparently, shelters under this cosmic umbrella. The 'iron cage' on the other hand, is how Max Weber, half a century earlier, described what replaces the sacred canopy in modern societies. Bureaucratic rationality, the quest of the most efficient way of organizing all human existence, threatened to displace all traces of the sacred canopy. At the same time, tasks which were previously the responsibility of the Church—such as education and welfare—were increasingly taken over by the state. It seemed that the sacred canopy simply became redundant.

It is not surprising that Victorian social commentators were so intrigued—and bewildered—by the changes overtaking society. The slow but steady transformation of agriculture and the revolution in 'industry' had a huge social impact. It was not merely that new scientific techniques were applied to agriculture and the production of commodities. Of course the steam engine was an amazing invention, but it was its effect in reducing labour requirements or transporting large numbers of people which made the deeper revolution. The changing techniques necessarily involved a huge shift away from the land, and the emergence of whole new classes of citizens, whose lives were increasingly geared to the nation-state, and who lived in the mushrooming urban areas of Europe. It seemed that a complete way of life was disappearing. In its place came growing factories, smoky cities, a new enthusiasm and prestige for science, labour unions, and the embryonic stirrings of democracy. One of the most crucial transformations involved the splitting apart of 'home' and 'work', and 'work' and 'leisure' as men and women forsook their 'domestic industry' and their farms to go 'out to work'. Thus people began to redefine work so that it became almost exclusively associated with paid employment.

What did these gigantic changes mean for human life? How had the modern world come into being? And what were its future prospects? These questions engaged the attention of a number of social thinkers who are now thought of as the pioneers of social science. They include Saint-Simon, Auguste Comte, Karl Marx, Alexis de Tocqueville, Max Weber, Ferdinand Tonnies, Emile Durkheim, and Sigmund Freud. Each in his way tried to grapple with the new pressing problems of the human condition in an industrial capitalist age. Friedrich Engels, for instance, saw London as a microcosm of the new age:

We know well enough that the isolation of the individual—a narrow-minded egotism—is everywhere the fundamental principle in modern society. But nowhere is this selfish egotism so blatantly evident as in the frantic bustle of the great city. The disintegration of society into individuals, each guided by his private principles and each pursuing his own aims, has been pushed to its furthest limits in London. Here indeed human society has been split into its component atoms. (Quoted in Kumar, 1978, p. 69)

Each sought to identify those factors which had ushered in the new society, the causes of disturbances and discontents which in some ways threatened it, and the discernible trends which would yield clues about society's future direction.

In so doing, each early social analyst noted the influence of religion in bringing about the new world, and each speculated on the likely fortunes of religion as industrial society matured. Durkheim, for instance, though he believed that 'as one advances in history, from inferior society to the city, from city to Christian peoples, one observes that religion withdraws more and more from public life' (Durkheim, 1958, p. 225), also felt this process was accelerating in industrial society. Thus, one could not hope to understand the modern world without reference to the fate of religion. Weber also felt that contemporary conditions were unique. He perceived an 'iron cage' forming around Western society, engulfing all life, including religion (1976, pp. 181—3). According to him, this cage was in part constructed as part of a response to Christian teachings, but was eventually destined to imprison those teachings. Marx, while he observed that rampant capitalist production was 'drowning the most heavenly ecstasies' of religious devotion, clearly saw no need for such ecstasies in his vision of future society (Marx and Engels, 1967, p. 82). Durkheim on the other hand, although he noted the 'contraction' of traditional religion, held out the hope that new social forms of religion would develop.

Religion is thus found near the core of early social studies of the modern world. No pioneer social thinker doubted for a moment the influence of religion on the formation of the modern world, or that contemporary social change involved religious change. One of the first to note this was Henri, Comte de Saint-Simon, who wrote with great enthusiasm of standing at the threshold of a new era in history. As a French aristocrat who had survived the 1789 revolution, and had watched the collapse of the established Church, he believed there was no future for Christianity as traditionally understood in France. But he did feel it necessary to propose some new religious basis on which the 'society of science' should rest. He even called it the 'New Christianity'. Echoes of this are found in the work of later social scientists. Although they pruned away the more exotic features of these 'new religions', there was a strong feeling that the corrosion of conventional Christianity would so weaken the social foundations that finding some alternative was imperative.

The almost overwhelming sense of previously unimaginable social transformation lay behind the intellectual attempt to account for these changes. As part of the modernizing movement entailed applying science to more and more areas of life, so many of these intellectuals groped towards a 'science of society'. Within these sciences of society, religion's role and future had a central place, and this is where the roots of secularization theory are to be found. Of course in a sense the science of society was not new; it depended heavily on previous historical ways of accounting for social change. And while it is a mistake to erect a disciplinary boundary between sociology and history, there is one prominent feature of nineteenth-century history which sociology could profitably have ignored. I refer to the use of the idea of evolution for explaining social change.

Secularization as an Evolutionary Process

Lifting the Darwinian idea of evolution from its biological context and attempting to apply it to society is one of the most popular and most mistaken ploys in the history of sociology. A prominent proponent of this was Victorian sage Herbert Spencer. He hoped to build the entire edifice of scientific sociology on what he felt was a firm foundation of evolutionary ideas. T. H. Huxley, who publicly championed Darwin, regarded Spencer as a vital ally in the battle of science against theology. And Darwin's hypothesis was also used as a buttress for the popular Victorian belief in progress. Reason, science and industry seemed visibly to confirm that progress was occurring. Darwin's theory, when applied broadly enough, could easily be pressed into service as a scientific rationale for 'progress'. If the 'fittest' survive in nature, why not also in society? If emergent species are 'superior' to previous ones (which through weakness become extinct), then why should not emergent forms of society also be superior? Industrialism and progress were, in Spencer's mind, virtually synonymous. Evolution underlay them both.

Edward Tylor, a founder of modern anthropology, also used the evolutionary idea in his study of 'primitive' peoples. Religion belonged to the primitive state, according to him. If somehow it appeared in the modern period, it was designated a 'survival'. Just as it was supposed that the coccyx is a vestigial remnant of a pre-human tail, so religion is also a hangover from a less civilized past. While there is, as far as I am aware, no evidence that Tylor advocated the surgical removal of monkeys' tails to discover whether this might hasten their human development, he did argue that the religious relics of a bygone era should be 'marked out for destruction' (Tylor 1871, p. 203; see also Burrow, 1966). Secularization for him as for others such as Durkheim and Marx was regarded as a policy as well as a description of religion in the modern world.

For Karl Marx, religion was an illusion. He saw it as a kind of symptom of social disorder which sustains and aggravates that disorder. It expresses pathological alienation. To attain social freedom and maturity, religion has to be shaken off. Marx thought of religion as a poor substitute for action, which would become obsolete as that (revolutionary) action came into its own, and as a society was born without the need for religion. Marx did acknowledge that religion could yield a sense of human self-awareness, and a means of interpreting the world. But he believed it to be mistaken and misleading. Religion obscured reality. When reality was unveiled, religion would be unnecessary.

Marxist historians still fall back on the evolutionary assumptions which underpin all Marx's theories of society. Eric Hobsbawm, for example, maintains that the decisive trend in Victorian religion was in a secularizing direction (despite some significant evidence of growth in some churches, and in the social impact of religion) (Hobsbawm, 1962, p. 261). The key metaphor, which gives the overall flavour, is that of secularization as an evolutionary process. David Martin cites this in his critique of secularization as an 'anti-religious ideology' (1965, p. 169). For the consistent orthodox Marxist the evolutionary element is still basic to social theory. Religion will be eliminated through the historical triumph of reason embodied in the social movement which finally ends all alienation.

Max Weber did not share Marx's outlook on this matter. Nevertheless, since Weber's turn-of-the-century writing his ideas on 'rationalization' have been implicitly linked up with evolutionary social thought. Weber believed that the power of religion was waning in the modern world under the impact of 'rationality', which was being extended into every human realm. So he thought of secularization very much as a by-product of rationalization. A certain spirit of inevitability pervades some of Weber's writing, which resonates all too easily with evolution. So although commentators like Durkheim and Spencer were much more explicitly evolutionary, some later sociologists saw them flowing together into one stream. Ex-Presbyterian minister Robert Lynd, co-author of the famous 1920s and 1930s studies of Middletown, USA, was one of these:

Like many other sociologists of his time, he viewed social evolution as an inevitable progression from social forms based on custom to social forms based on rational planning. According to this view, drawn from nineteenth-century extensions of Darwin's discussion of the origin of species to social institutions, modern religion was supposed to be a vestige of a more primitive stage of society and was expected to disappear. This gradual but inevitable disappearance was called secularization. (Caplow, 1984, p. 106)

What these evolutionary notions of secularization have in common is that they are distanced from social reality.

As mentioned in chapter 1, the general critique of evolutionism in sociology and Marxism centres on its denigration of human agents. People are perceived as pawns in the game of 'massive social forces'. In its early forms, evolutionary theory put stress on social 'laws' which, it was supposed, could be discovered in much the same way as

29

'laws' of physics (see Smith, 1976, pp. 32−8). From the present perspective, such 'laws' are little more than social 'trends' or 'tendencies'. They are inherently mutable and unstable, because they refer to reflexive human agents (see Lyon, 1983a; Giddens, 1979, p. 232).

When applied to secularization, evolutionary theory assumes that religion atrophies in the modern world. This in turn assumes that religion may be treated as a mere surface phenomenon whose constitution changes in response to deeper movements in society. Social adaptation (a process analogous to biological adaptation) is thought to occur in a mechanical fashion, behind people's backs, as it were. I am not for a moment suggesting that people and institutions do not adapt themselves to altered social circumstances. Of course they do. The trouble with the evolutionary analogy lies in its misleading tendency to downplay the role of reflexive human beings within that adaptation process.

Evolutionary theories of secularization also exude an air of inevitability about the fate of religion. The secularization process, once set in train, is likely to continue unchecked into the future. For the Victorian era, evolutionary interpretations of social change served as a handy catch-all at a time when older, providentialist interpretations seemed less plausible. Although this was not always the case, for this reason secularization theory often contained a strong dose of secularism.

Secularization and Secularism

Secularization and secularism are not the same thing. Weber's discussion of the place of religion in the modern world − though he described himself as 'religiously tone-deaf'− is not overtly hostile towards religion. For some, secularization is a policy. This is secularism, whose tenets are set out most clearly by the Victorian founder of the secularist movement, G. J. Holyoake. To quote him: 'Science is the sole Providence of man, morals are independent of Christianity, men should trust Reason, and fair and open discussion, as the highest guarantee of public truth' (quoted in Campbell, 1971, p. 47).

Secularization represents a social scientific attempt to capture in one word a complex social process. It has to do with the relationship between religion and society. Generally, religion is seen in some way to be losing out within secularization theory. But the social analyst or historian describing secularization may do so with regret or by way of a warning. Secularism exhibits no regret about religion's supposed decline. On the contrary, secularism is a set of beliefs and practices committed to the abolition of religion in society. Religion is viewed in an uncompromisingly negative light. But just as secularization studies may be carried out from the standpoint of a Christian sympathizer, they may also be done by a committed secularist. So it is not always a simple matter to separate secularization from secularism, even though the two are logically distinct.

In fact, secularization has strong connotations of 'enlightenment' which persist to this day. As Owen Chadwick observes, if 'enlightenment' was the word used by an intellectual élite who proclaimed themselves free from prejudice and superstition, then 'secularization' was often thought of as the extension of enlightenment to the 'masses' (Chadwick, 1975, p. 9). The spirit of the French Enlightenment, the quest of rationally-based free enquiry, without 'theology', spread far beyond the French border. Isaiah Berlin says that the Enlightenment thinkers believed that 'all the sciences and faiths . . . when "cleansed" of their irrational elements by the advance of civilization, can be harmonized in the final true philosophy which could solve all theoretical and practical problems for all men everywhere for all time' (Berlin, 1956, p. 28). This view, though not always expressed with such unbounded optimism, still pervades 'modern' thought. 'Perhaps the most significant aspect of what it means to be modern', says secularization sociologist Bryan Wilson, 'is the idea that we can consciously change the character of society and the condition of our lives' (Wilson, 1976, p. 1). We return to this theme later.

The point at issue here, however, is that secularization studies may express a particular outlook or world-view which is opposed to religion. As 'secularization' is incorporated into social science usage (and is taken for granted as part of our description of the modern world), its 'enlightenment' connotations may get blurred and obscured. The idea that religion must decline in the modern world is a product of enlightenment-type thinking. Thomas Luckmann rightly objects that such hidden philosophies of history and unexamined perspectives on religion affect the whole social research process

(1977). They lead to pre-judgements about the relevance and irrelevance of data which could mean that in the end the sociological accounts could be very misleading.

Bryan Wilson acknowledges that some sociologies of secularization have been affected by such covert assumptions, but he excludes Durkheim and Weber from such a charge. Yet this is hardly warranted. Durkheim explicitly sought a new secular morality for France, to be built on the basis of sociology. He was a 'laicist' defender of the Third French Republic, and thus opposed the Church as being politically reactionary (Birnbaum and Lenzer, 1969, p. 10). Weber, on the other hand, although he regretted aspects of what he saw as the decline of religion, argued that this had to be accepted as a fact of modern life. To the religionists of his day he insisted that the rationalization process would permit no religious revival (Gerth and Mills, 1958, p. 155). Thus even Weber's relatively ironic approach is by no means neutral. This serves to demonstrate not only that secularization studies may be affected by explicit enlightenment secularism of a brash sort, but also that more subtle background assumptions may lie behind secularization theory. No matter how heavily these may be cloaked in the paraphernalia of social science jargon, or how acceptable is the sociologist in question as a 'founding father', such assumptions can hardly fail to skew the resulting social analysis.

Happily, today there exists a more widespread recognition of the importance of such background assumptions. Fewer social scientists would be willing to assert, as American post-war sociologist Kingsley Davis did, that religion 'withers like a leaf before a flame' when exposed to scientific scrutiny (1948, p. 536). But as Robert Bellah indicated in a now classic paper, 'Between Religion and Social Science', religious assumptions always intrude into studies of religion (1970). This is especially true of basic definitions; in the case of secularization studies, those relating to 'religion' and 'history'. Atheism, whether 'methodological' or not, is unnecessary to proper social science. In what follows we shall both attempt to expose the background assumptions of the theories examined, and also to explore what happens when other assumptions are allowed to enter social analysis.

Uncoupling Church and Society
Right from the start of his academic career, Emile Durkheim

was interested in the problem of religion in the modern world. Although Durkheim's most famous book on religion — *The Elementary Forms of the Religious Life* — did not appear until 1912, his concern with the social explanation of religion is evident much earlier. In his doctoral dissertation, published as *The Division of Labour in Society,* he wrote that

If there is a truth that history teaches us beyond doubt, it is that religion tends to embrace a smaller and smaller sector of social life. Originally it pervades everything; everything social is religious. The two words are synonymous. Then political, economic and scientific functions gradually free themselves from religious control, establish themselves separately and take on a more and more openly temporal character. (Quoted in Giddens, 1972, p. 245)

This is the process that I am referring to as the 'uncoupling of Church and society'. Durkheim is really pointing to two processes here. In the first, official church religion is systematically split away from other areas of society such as the economy. For instance, the medieval Catholic doctrine of the 'just price' was intended to ensure fair trading in the market place, so that no one was overcharged. But in the course of social development economic life was increasingly assumed to be independent of church control. In fact, the doctrine of *'laissez-faire'* meant that the economy should be freed of any external control, from whatever source.

The second aspect of the above quotation points to the actual transferral of some religious task or teaching into the 'secular' sphere. Society itself is seen to take over some of the functions previously thought of as being 'religious'. They become a purely human responsibility. Thus some government-controlled prices and incomes policy could be seen as the transposing into a secular key of that which was formerly religious.

Durkheim also had an explanation for this shift. For him, the contraction of religion

did not begin at some certain moment of history; we can follow its development from the earliest phases of social evolution. It is thus linked to the fundamental conditions of the development of societies, and this shows that there is a decreasing number of collective beliefs and sentiments which are both collective and strong enough to assume a religious character. (Quoted in Giddens, 1972, p. 245)

The quotation reveals Durkheim's commitment to evolutionary explanation, and also his view that religion is in a sense a surface phenomenon whose fortunes are largely dictated by profound social change occuring in a deeper social layer.

Durkheim took this analysis further in *The Elementary Forms.* The social scientist, according to Durkheim, must assume the naturalness of all phenomena. If a rite or symbol is observed, then it is assumed that it refers to a human need. The sociologist has to discover that need in order to explain the phenomenon. Durkheim held that if only one could find the most primitive form of the rite, symbol or belief, then one could explain it. This conviction led him to study what had been written about the central Australian Arunta tribe of aborigines. When this isolated people met, they performed rites around a totem. The totem was a respected plant or other object. The sacred things were organized into a system and separated from the 'profane' reality of everyday life. This gave the clan an identity, said Durkheim, and also a sense of unity. So here was the 'need' met by their religion; it served to yield a sense of social cohesion. As society became more sophisticated, philosophical and later scientific categories would be derived from religion.

Durkheim was saying that religion can be explained by referring to society: it is an entirely social phenomenon. If the social scientist peeps behind the religious façade, society itself is found. As Durkheim said, 'If religion has given birth to all that is essential to society, it is therefore society that is the soul of religion'. Religion also serves society in other related ways. It gives strength to endure life. It has a disciplinary function in that its sanctions, which originate beyond everyday life, contribute to social control in the community. And it also generates a sense of well-being. The act of coming together at a funeral, for example, provides a sense of togetherness which cements the group together after its loss.

Such observations have become commonplace in Western societies today; they pass as 'social scientific'. But they are not without problems. For a start, Durkheim seemed to be setting up science as the arbiter of religion. Science discovers the true secret of the meaning of religion in society itself. Nevertheless, society 'needs' religion in order to function properly. But, how scientific was Durkheim? Was his sample not rather limited? Who says that the Arunta are the 'most primitive' tribe? Why should the functions of religion isolated by Durkheim be thought of as the primary or manifest ones?

It is unfortunate, to put it mildly, that many who have read Durkheim (or Freud for that matter, whose explanations of religion are not dissimilar) assume that he has in some way explained away religion. But the arguments about the 'social functions of religion', or about societies' 'needs' for religion are notoriously slipshod. If by 'function' is meant 'consequence', such that religion's social consequence is a greater sense of group cohesion, then this might tell us a little about the circumstances under which religion persists, but nothing about the origin, still less about the truth of religion. And if the idea of 'need' is brought in, or if 'function' is used as 'purpose' ('the purpose of religion is to bring about social cohesion') then this is simply illegitimate. Societies cannot have purposes; only individual human beings can. This form of objection in no way damages the claim that the actions of human beings have (frequently unforeseen) consequences which then constrain future actions of those or other humans. In this sense one might even talk of social 'forces'; certainly of 'social structure'. To take a popular Marxist type of argument, one could say that religion may be a social force for political control. This may indeed reveal some (intended or unintended) consequences of religion, but it in no way explains the presence or origin of religion, as is sometimes implied.

Another question, following on from our discussion of the 'functions' of religion, relates to what Durkheim omitted. All his functions of religion are essentially conservative. They serve the *status quo* rather than in any sense catalysing change or standing against dominant social currents. Yet plenty of evidence exists (some of which is examined by Max Weber) for religion as an agent of social transformation. And when a William Wilberforce or a Martin Luther King does initiate social movement based on some kind of 'prophetic' social critique, can their activities really be explained away in the social terms to which Durkheim was committed? There does seem to be some circular reasoning here, originating in Durkheim's insistence on the ultimacy of social forces in determining the outcomes of social situations.

But whatever the shortcomings and faults of Durkheim's views, much work in the sociology of religion has been based on foundations he laid. Certain insights have been woven into more general theories of religion-and-society, and these have come to form part of the agenda for secularization studies.

Durkheim was convinced about the disappearance of conventional religion with the maturing of industrialism. For him, religious beliefs express the character of social totality. So trouble was bound to come when society was atomized by new industrial and productive processes. Under such conditions religion as he saw it could only loosen its grip on the routines of everyday life. Thus the old deities would certainly disappear.

But his argument was not ultimately related to industrialism as such. Like Weber, he saw the breakup of medievalism (as Church-and-state partnership) as the cause lying behind secularizing movements of industrial society. When Renaissance leaders, steeped in Greek and Roman thought, put humans rather than God at the centre of the universe, this was a decisive step in the direction of individualism (which of course comes into its own in industrial capitalism). This movement was reinforced, said Durkheim, by the Reformation's denial of the church's authority, and its insistence on the authority of the Bible to the individual conscience.

Secularization in Durkheim's France was illustrated, as he saw it, by a number of factors. Church and state were finally sundered by the anti-clerical Third Republic in 1905, clearly showing the Church's loss of temporal power. Sacred religion allowed itself to be profaned by scientific inquiry, which would formerly have been denounced as anathema by the Roman Catholic Church. Similarly, Durkheim felt French society to be secular because it tolerated sacrilege. No one bothered any more about public defamation of the Church. Moreover, in other ways people were a law to themselves, bowing to no religious authority, especially if they, like Durkheim himself, were members of the university intelligentsia (see Pickering, 1984, pp. 448—51). Science has an intrinsically secularizing tendency.

Still, Durkheim did offer the hope that new social forms of religion more appropriate to industrial society would emerge, despite the fact that truth is ultimately to be found in science! He predicted that new ideals of moral individualism, which, he declared, exhibited a religious character, would re-integrate societies fragmented by industrialism. His real desire, clearly, was for a social ethic dependent on Christian capital, but shorn of its spiritual dimension. In so doing Durkheim aligned himself with the growth of modern humanism which, as he correctly observed, had accompanied the decline of traditional religion.

Disenchanting the World

Max Weber, unlike Durkheim, expressed no note of optimism about religion. In 1918 he gave a famous lecture to his students. Entitled *Science as a Vocation,* it took the form of a candid statement of Weber's hopes and fears for intellectual life in the West. It has a close bearing on the secularization theme and indeed on all the rest of Weber's work. As he put it: 'the fate of our times is intellectualization, rationalization and the disenchantment of the world' (Gerth and Mills, 1958, p. 155).

Intellectualization, a process Weber said had been going for millennia, in the modern world takes the form of science and technology. This does not mean that all know more about life (because more people are specialists). But it does mean that in principle there are no incalculable forces. All things, theoretically, may be mastered through calculation. There is less recourse to magic. The sacred, if that is associated with the unknowable, occupies diminishing space.

Science increases the sphere of the quantifiable—things which can be measured and counted. It allows for experimentation. It gives us concepts. For Puritans at the threshold of modern science, it even provided a way of knowing the Creator. Ironically, science became irreligious, or at least divorced from the meaning it was thought to reveal. Weber sympathetically quoted Tolstoy's complaint that science is meaningless because it gives us no clues as to how we should live. Even social science, says Weber, can only set the options before us; it cannot prescribe the right course of action. This is the root of the modern *malaise,* for Weber. Science has been elevated to a social pinnacle, but all it can give us is clarification of problems and some knowledge of how facts relate to each other. This is disenchantment: 'sublime values' have retreated from public life.

For Weber, this meant that no ultimate meaning is ever possible. Within science, the proliferation of disciplines leads to a fragmentation of knowledge. This is mirrored in life in general. There is no unifying *'gestalt'*, no single vision, no prophets. No one can agree the priorities for evaluating life: each simply 'follows the demon which holds the fibres of his very life'. So Weber's view of secularization involves a pessimistic resignation to competition between individual values within a plural society.

Thus Weber was caught in a classic bind of modern Western society. Science seems to liberate us from necessity by providing the means of conquering nature. But it is a pyrrhic victory, for science then enshackles us in a world without any real meaning. And as he observed the early phases of German industry, and the slow-grinding Teutonic bureaucracy, he could see that already its routines served to deepen that meaninglessness. He attributed to this the younger generation's 'ubiquitous chase for "experience" ' (1948, p. 149).

Weber was concerned, more than were Durkheim or Marx, with the *meaning* of action. So his sociology of religion, which has meaning at its core, is vital to the rest of his social— historical theory. Modern society is pervaded by rationaliza- tion, the hallmark of which is a calculating, amoral approach to human problems which progressively invades all of life. In the economy this spells the birth of capitalism. In political life, rationalization is seen in the growth of bureaucracy. Culturally, rationalization means the rising social significance of science and the declining social significance of religion. As Philip Abrams has it: 'Secularization gives rise to a science- dominated culture in which whatever is "scientific" is valued regardless of its social effects, and only what is science is accepted and esteemed as knowledge' (1982, p. 84). This is what Weber feared as the 'iron cage'.

Weber's best-known book is *The Protestant Ethic and the Spirit of Capitalism.* With the other founding fathers of social science, his desire was to discover the roots of the modern world. So he explored the kind of economic practice involved in capitalism (rather than just looking at the kinds of relationships it generated, as Marx had done). For instance, he saw the innovation of double-column accounting as a key moment in the rationalizing of economic life. He never argued (as some have mistakenly believed him to have done) that Protestantism had some kind of prior orientation towards capitalism. On the contrary, he showed by various quotations from Wesley and others that Protestantism was actually opposed to some aspects of what we now think of as capitalist practice. Rather, certain unintended consequences of Christian teaching—especially about the 'calling'—contributed indirectly to capitalism's growth. The Protestant struggle to emancipate believers from the power of the Roman Catholic Church served in the end to create a world of meaning which freed capitalism from economic tradition.

John Wesley in fact recognized the seeming paradox that Methodists were, due to their diligence and frugality, becoming rich. He saw the results of this in pride and unsatiated appetite: 'the continual decay of pure religion' (Weber 1976, p. 175). But while he could see the negative consequences of teaching frugality and diligence as Christian virtues, he could see no alternative but to continue teaching what he knew to be true.

Ironically then, Protestantism, with its inbuilt antipathy to luxurious lifestyles and to self-centred gain, came to be viewed as the seed-bed for a capitalist system which embodied just those aspects. Accumulation for its own sake seemed to be a capitalist rule, whereas Protestantism, as Weber pointed out, seemed if anything to lean in the direction of asceticism. This is one of the ways in which, it is said, Protestantism became its own gravedigger. It illustrates both the secularization of economics and the way in which this secularization has wider social implications. The spirit of capitalism requires no justification beyond that of the profit motive, and it tends to subsume other (social and cultural) goals under that justification.

Weber also noted the process of rationalization in science. He maintained that the rise of modern science could only be a threat to traditional religion. His work has helped give rise to a cultural myth, that science somehow pushes religion out of the picture. As Susan Budd has suggested, part of science's apparent superiority lies in its achievements in controlling nature, but part also lies in the myth about 'the clash between religion and science which was resolved in favour of science' (1973, p. 143). As with all myths, this one does have its origins in symbolic events of note. A public battle of 'science versus religion' was waged in Victorian England, while similar symbolic battles were fought elsewhere.

Throughout the 1870s the influential English periodicals (themselves enjoying an unprecedented boom in popularity as a medium for national debate) carried articles which chronicle this 'victory of science' and the 'crisis of faith'. And, in a similar way to which pre-Enlightenment religion was discredited by the loss of church power and prestige rather than by arguments against its teaching, Victorian religion lost more because of who controlled the journals than because of decisive arguments against the truth or morality of Christianity. The periodical press was in the hands of atheists and agnostics who were keen to show how religion was superfluous to modern life. This is not to say that people did not have their moral and logical arguments. They did (Budd, 1977). The point is that the myth of the triumph of science over religion was *socially* established.

Another thing which was socially established during this period was the idea of a 'new priesthood' of science. Auguste Comte had mooted this in France much earlier in the century, but for various reasons it took longer to catch on in Britain. In fact, although many talked about the development of a 'clerisy' of scientists to take over where theologians had left off — Durkheim himself advocated something like this in France — nothing was formally established. But a century later the authority of science and scientists has become dominant. From the classroom to the TV show, science has high prestige. Even those who might once have appealed to revelation in matters cosmological now appeal to science to support 'creation' (see for example Barker, 1980). It is only since the 1960s that serious voices have been raised in protest against scientism and technocracy.

There are grounds, then, for accepting at least part of Weber's thesis about the rationalization and thus the secularization of the modern world. Capitalism, science and bureaucracy furnish us with plenty of illustrations of this putative process. But there are also plenty of loose ends and question marks. Weber's legacy is something of a 'cultural bathtub' — a picture of society which has science being poured in, while religion slops out over the sides.

One problem with this is simply that late twentieth-century advanced societies still contain much superstition, magic and mythology. Moreover, as David Martin reminds us, technologically sophisticated societies are capable of holding to crass belief systems: 'The perverse transcendence of the American way of life, the cult of royalty or the threadbare eschatology and diseased vocabulary of Marxist aspiration is an index of the fantastic gullibility of modern man' (1969, p. 114).

Another problem relates to the meaning of 'rationalization' and 'rationality'. Weber was in fact aware of the subtle nuances of meaning here, and yet gave the impression that the *instrumental* rationality (for example of the bureaucracy) was dominant in the modern world. But why did he regard religion as 'irrational'? There seems to be an inconsistency here. For religion, according to him, contributed to the 'de-magic-ing' of nature, making it amenable to scientific investigation. It also gives a stable interpretation of social, individual and natural reality which, according to the *Protestant Ethic* thesis, helped produce the distinctive characteristics of the modern world.

Such questions are issues which all secularization studies encounter. We confront them in later chapters of the book. Their existence is part of the reason why it is necessary to go beyond secularization for an adequate understanding of religion and contemporary society.

Religion was central to the work of the pioneers of social science. Durkheim and Weber both recognized the importance of religion in the forming of the modern world, and speculated about religion's future in their secularizing societies. Their insights have an abiding relevance today. Take Durkheim's penetrating observations about the roots of modern individualism lying in the human displacing of God from the centre of the universe. This forms a vital background to the contemporary 'dethronement of man', in which now even humans are supplanted. Without the notion of a Creator, human uniqueness is also eroded. Similarly, Weber's eye for the interlocking ironies of the historical drama still gives good guidance. The perverse pattern of events persists today in which Christianity's contribution to the rise of modern science and capitalism rebounds to undermine it. The Church permits its performance to be measured by the very criteria of that science, technology and capitalism, rather than those of its charter documents.

At the same time, our use of such insights has to be tempered by caution. The analysis of these tremendous social transformations emerged from their very midst, so it is hardly surprising that attitudes current at the time—such as evolutionism—came to be embedded in that analysis. Thus it is that secularism and secularization are not so easily disentangled. And even if the social analysts in question were not overtly hostile to religion, this does not mean that their studies were somehow entirely neutral. The weighing of the evidence for or against the secularization story is always done in the light of certain crucial assumptions.

3: The Secularization Story

> 'Religion has been converted from the keystone which holds together the social edifice into one department within it, and the idea of a rule of right is replaced by economic expediency as the arbiter of policy and the criterion of conduct.' (R. H. Tawney, *Religion and the Rise of Capitalism,* first published 1926)

Drawing on a number of commentators from both sides of the Atlantic, this chapter describes the main contours of today's 'secular' landscape. People's thinking takes God or religion less into account. Local communities, which, Tawney suggests once had religion as their bondstone, have broken up, with the effect that the role of the Church has also come up for grabs, especially in urban environments. The state and other authorities have shaken off their erstwhile reliance on religion, leaving ways of life to individual whim or bureaucratic regulation. The Church has been relegated to the margins of society, and religion has become essentially a private affair.

All this has consequences for society. For instance, the sharply felt crises of political legitimacy or personal identity are related to these aspects of secularization. We think that we can create by our own unaided efforts the kind of society or people that we want. We believe that we can find technical solutions to our problems. Acts of Parliament or parking meters will answer all.

But there are also consequences for the Church, which are hinted at here, but to which we also return later. Religion no longer enjoys state support. Science and technological exploits are sometimes thought to challenge belief in God's providence. Christianity is one 'way' among others which may or may not be equally valid. Christian people learn to live with the situation in which religion may be vital to their personal existence but apparently irrelevant to the workings of the 'real world' out there.

So the coming of modernity means that the writing is on the church wall. Contemporary urban society is simply inhospitable to religion. In today's hi-tech world, Christian belief, or faith of any sort, is rendered difficult or impossible. The rapidly dwindling domains of the Church spell the death of institutional Christianity.

The foregoing phrases are caricatures of course. They oversimplify the situation. Yet such popular clichés did not appear from nowhere. Many serious commentators used expressions like this to sum up the religious condition of 'modernity'. The secularization story made sense of such assertions, and put them in an overall explanatory framework. Building on the foundation laid by the classical sociologists, secularization's story-tellers wove together themes of urbanization, technical sophistication and the takeover of 'religious' tasks by other agencies, into a pattern which is by now fairly well-known. Religion is on its way out. Society has developed ways of coping without the help of Christianity.

Later on, we shall see that most of today's sociologists and historians are more careful. They hesitate before making global pronouncements about the fate of religion in society. Peter Berger, for instance, whose contribution to the secularization debate in the 1970s was so seminal, now has deep doubts about how far secularization can go. But while the secularization story may be slipping from prominence at the frontiers of social research, it is by no means out of favour in the media, in textbooks and in popular assumption.

Let us begin with Berger. He focuses on the secularizing of social structure, but also, more especially, on the 'secularization of consciousness' in the modern world. Individuals increasingly look on their lives, he says, without the benefit of a religious interpretation (1969, p. 108). The person in business or commerce is pursuing the most profitable course, not necessarily the most ethical or socially beneficial. Sexual feelings, as Ernest Troeltsch once noted, are severed from any doctrine such as 'original sin', which might hint that sex may be misdirected as well as enjoyed responsibly (Troeltsch, 1958, p. 96). Children are accepted into the family, not as gifts received according to God's timing, but as the products of careful planning and so-called birth control. And education is sought, not in relation to some criterion of truth or wisdom, but rather to be in tune with today's industrial 'requirements'.

Berger sees this kind of shift in thinking as the result of a 'package' of 'modernity' which is currently being exported throughout the world. Modernity includes scientific and technological approaches to problems, an industrial base, bureaucratic government institutions and expanding communications media. Modernity has already had a huge impact in the West, and is now making its mark in the so-called developing nations. The traditional meaningful order of social life is disrupted, social life is split into 'public' and 'private' sectors, and novel attractions such as nationalism and socialism appear. People no longer feel 'at home', having lost their familiar, traditional environment. In short, says Berger, 'homeless minds' multiply (1974).

This is illuminating, but there is little doubt that its effect is first felt (though not necessarily recognized) in the churches. As far back as 1952 a British commentator, Stephen Spinks, issued this doleful report:

In the years that followed the war, ministers of many denominations who had hoped for a 'return to religion' experienced periods of great depression. Many a devoted parish priest . . . who had spent the greater part of his ministerial life in one area and had been robbed by air-raids and evacuation both of church and congregation, found his life's work brought to a calamitous end. The 'return to religion' did not come' (Spinks, 1952).

Church buildings became derelict, or had other uses found for them (such as warehousing or, following waves of Asian immigration in the 1960s, as temples and mosques). According to 'Mass Observation' people prayed less, or used only childhood rote prayers. The BBC opened itself to broadcasting opinions hostile to Christianity for the first time. Religion seemed to have a decreasing place in national life, unless one counts prayer at the beginning of the parliamentary session. Certainly the calls to prayer which had once been issued by government in times of national crisis, such as harvest failure or war, have become a thing of the past. The clergy also have been stripped, more and more, of their previous role. 'Professional' counsellors, therapists, and social workers are turned to instead. For the majority of one's waking hours, especially in paid employment, one is exposed to, and expected to operate according to, criteria which have no religious sanction and which may in fact be inimical to Christian teaching and practice. Efficiency, productivity and profitability hardly count as virtues in themselves.

All this is seen by many as bad news for the churches. For Bryan Wilson, that is very much what secularization is all about: bad news for the churches. And as religion is, for him, almost entirely bound up with institutional fortunes, this kind of data indicates the decline of religion in modern society. But can we be certain that there really is a discernible trend towards 'religious decline', and if there is, that it should be interpreted in this fashion? This, of course, is the nub of the question addressed in this book.

The kind of evidence used must plainly be of tremendous significance. Just because, for example, the British BBC admits all comers to the religious debate, this does not necessarily mean a fall-off in religious interest. Peak-time 'Songs of Praise' still goes out each Sunday, and controversy within the Church of England is still accorded TV time. Moreover, TV can change—and is changing. Preachers as 'personalities' attract millions of viewers in the USA, are picking up a following in Canada, and hope to use TV channels opened up by cabling in Britain in the near future.

To take another example where discretion must be used, the declining national clout of the clergy is by no means terminal. Without remarking on the more blatant and commonplace interventions in American politics in the name of religion (as seen for example in the Mondale/Reagan battle for the White House in 1984), one also finds similar evidence on the European side of the Atlantic. Ecclesiastical resistance to war-glorifying thanksgiving services provoked government concern in Britain following the Falklands débâcle in 1982. And in 1984 the Bishop of Durham's enthronement speech, in which he criticized the importing of an American National Coal Board chief during the delicate moments of the miners' strike, caused something approaching senior ministerial apoplexy, and opened a new chapter in the 'altar and throne' controversy. The same bishop has achieved notoriety for his allegedly heretical views on the virgin birth and the resurrection, and these, too, have been considered newsworthy.

All I intend, by introducing such apparently contradictory data at this point, is to counsel caution. The point of this chapter is not to confuse the reader but rather to outline the main features of the secularization story. Leaving aside for the moment the more eccentric and now faded claims about the overall 'secularization of consciousness' in modern societies, or the notion that shifting institutional church fortunes means the entire evacuation of religion from the world, we may usefully focus on more modest proposals. Some of the regularly-used raw materials of the secularization story do indeed bear comment and invite explanation.

Historians and social analysts have come up with some generalizations about the experiences of religion in the modern world. David Martin lists a number of these for us (1978, pp. 2, 3). Where heavy industry is found, religious institutions tend to lose support proportionately to the rest of the population, especially when relative 'working class' density is high. There seems to be proportionately less overt religious practice in big cities than in more sparsely populated regions. Jobs and careers which require movement away from stable religious communities, especially when they have a territorial base, hasten the break up of those communities. Greater culture-contact, which is a frequent effect of such movement, opens people to new ideas and lifestyles, and can lead to a radical questioning of once-accepted verities. Churches tend to be split into a variety of denominations and sects, thus weakening any visible unity which may have been present with a single established institution. And lastly, the churches are themselves cut loose from involvement in the processes of justice, legitimation, the state, social control, education and welfare. At the same time, individuals' everyday lives are more compartmentalized, which encourages further differences in personal religion and thus amplifies the disintegration process within the institutions.

Community-Lost?
Secularization is the inevitable consequence of the breakdown of traditional communities. This is a recurring theme of secularization studies (and the first of three examined here).

Bryan Wilson has a technical term for the process: societalization. By this he means that a characteristic of the modern world is the way we live our lives in relation to a big social system. Gone are the daily face-to-face contacts of work, and interdependence with neighbour and kin in the stable agricultural community. In their place, the anonymity of relationships with bus-driver and bank-teller, which are all part of a wider network of intermeshed social, political and economic relationships within what we know as the nation state. Societalization spells both loss-of-community and secularization.

There is something to this secularization as 'community-lost' idea. Evidence from nineteenth-century England, for example, shows that the collapse of traditional communities in the wake of expanding capitalist agriculture did indeed have a strong bearing on what happened to the churches. James Obelkelvitch's investigation of rural Lincolnshire illustrates this well (1976). The older peasant-style community involved subsistence, co-operation, common land, self-policing with locally-administered moral sanctions and more face-to-face relationships than in modern times, including many significant ones outside the immediate family. Vertical ties of deference from below, and paternalism from above, were the order of things. The labourer would touch his forelock to the landowner, who would in turn inquire after the health of the labourer's family, on the basis of personal knowledge. As James Southey wrote in 1820, each parish was a 'little commonwealth' (quoted in Gilbert 1980, p. 81).

However, rapidly changing patterns of land-ownership linked with the attempt to turn farming into a profitable capitalist enterprise, put an end to all this. The landowners withdrew from the community, forming their own class. Smallholders were squeezed, and the numbers of landless rose. Farmers grew rich, and adopted what we would now loosely call a middle-class lifestyle. The harvest supper — so well depicted in Thomas Hardy's *Far from the Madding Crowd* — became a mere memory (or was subverted as a means of social control).

All this meant considerable changes for the churches in Lincolnshire. The Church of England, already somewhat remote from those who worked the land, received another setback with the shift towards capitalism. It came to be more associated with the new landowning class; its clergy were, after all, 'gentlemen'. While a traditional deference of workers to clergy continued, the same workers were very attracted to nonconformist religion. Methodism formed an alternative source of social support when the community began to erode. As one worker told an Anglican clergyman, 'We goes to church to please you, sir, and to chapel at night to save our souls'. Methodism, with its emphasis on simplicity, discipline and adherence to the Bible, seemed to many a much more authentic version of Christianity than the culturally remote ruminations of the largely absentee parish priest.

But this is all part of the secularization story: religion being steadily weakened by internal splits. Obelkevitch's own rather heavy conclusion is that in a class society, as opposed to community, secularization was pretty well unavoidable. Without 'community' support, both superstitious and Christian religion was bound to fade.

Nonetheless, the differences made by industrialism are often exaggerated. As the Lincolnshire example shows, the economic changes which contributed to the disintegration of local communities and thus to traditional religion, may in some cases have strengthened some religious movements, such as Methodism. After all, in the earlier industrial period preachers John Wesley and George Whitefield concentrated their efforts on cities such as Newcastle, Bristol and London. At the same time, the attractions of chapel could have had long-term disadvantages, for some nonconformists built on their success at attracting those made insecure in a more fragmented society by providing leisure-time recreational activities. When competition came from other, 'secular' sources, this was detrimental to the chapels (see Cox, 1982).

The other side of the 'community-lost' coin is, of course, urbanization. For many—not least contemporary theologians like Harvey Cox—urbanism epitomizes modernity. In the hands of the inheritors of the European legacy of social theorizing, urbanism came to be seen as the polar opposite of community. So when American or, later, Canadian researchers began examining their own drift from the land, they anticipated the breakdown of community and thus also of religion and morality (for example, Stein, 1960). A rather crude before-and-after picture of the transformation to industrial capitalist society held sway. The category 'religion' belonged with 'before' items, such as tradition and agriculture, whereas the category 'secular' belonged to the 'after' section, along with science and industry.

To show how urbanism is hostile to certain traditional forms of religious organization is simply not the same as showing how urbanism is hostile to religion as such. In any case, 'urbanism' is not only found in big cities. What we are really talking about is an aspect of a wider phenomenon which has as much to do with an industrial or commercial outlook as it does with housing density. For the countryside has today been 'urbanized', just as farming has become mechanized and capitalist.

This is not to say no change has occurred; far from it. The interdependent, multi-faceted social groupings of yesteryear have in large part given way to more partial associations of people who are only together for a limited purpose — such as a labour union or a neighbourhood playgroup. And it is true to say that the churches (and chapels!) have not shown themselves particularly adept at responding to this modern, pluralist situation.

In fact, (middle-class) churches often resemble not the all-round relationships of 'community', but social groupings that classical sociologist Ferdinand Tonnies saw as typical of modernity: 'associations'. They restrict themselves to one limited purpose, which is why their social action has frequently been quite uncontroversial. Today this is changing, and perhaps the most pressing question for churches who do wish to be a rounded community of faith, touching the world at many points, is how far unity and biblical faithfulness can be maintained when more contentious issues — such as nuclear weaponry — are being faced.

Church liturgies, once linked with the natural rhythm of the seasons, have not kept pace (even if it is thought they should) with the flexible variety of modern society. It is not surprising that rural nostalgia is found among some churchpeople. The older professionalism, with its ties to place and people, has given way to a spiralling career pattern. It also absorbs more time and energy which might in another age have been given to the Church. Again, new leisure and travel opportunities mean less commitment to place. This may be because people are absent on trips or vacations (in parts of North America, the 'cottage' is the family rendezvous for several summer months on end), or because they are passive in front of the television. As David Martin says, we are often either mobile in cars or immobile before the television.

No wonder Wilson is pessimistic. He holds that religion has its source in, and draws its strength from, the local community (1976b). Nowadays society, not community, is the context in which people live their lives. As Tonnies and Durkheim predicted, the very assumptions by which society operates are secular. *Ergo,* religion must die.

Unfortunately, while the 'community-lost' idea does alert us to some of the dynamics of secularization, it can all too easily degenerate into a misplaced nostalgia for imagined times past, and thus befog analysis. As it happens, community persists in the modern world, even if 'society' does function according to bureaucratic rules. Moreover, older, local communities were not simply 'irrational'. They had their own logic, only not that of technique. And just as that logic lives on, so does that of religion. Life-crises and the empty routines of everyday existence throw up questions which admit of no merely temporal, calculating response (on this, see Luckmann, 1976).

Not only the backward-looking apprehension of past society but also the forward-looking assessment of present society may be distorted by 'community-lost' thinking. The purpose of the pioneer sociologists was not nostalgia, but to get to grips with contemporary society. What is occurring in the modern world is much more than a mere move from local community to nation state. Human beings are always stretching their social relationships over time and space. Transnational corporations and new telecommunications channels are contributing to an increasingly rapid *globalization* process. We are steadily sucked, like it or not, into a *world* system of politics and economics, which has a strong bearing on cultural and religious change (see Robertson, 1982; Wuthnow, 1982). What, for instance, will be the consequence of direct religious broadcasting by satellite, which beams some 'gospel' from a very remote culture into our living rooms? Also, humanity itself is today threatened by hunger and holocaust; this too raises religious questions.

The 'community-lost' thesis offers some significant clues as to why religious institutions have changed over the past century and a half. But it is also misleading. It exaggerates the differences between 'old' and 'new' society, and diverts attention from other tendencies, such as the influence of *world* history on religion in a given society. The ancient local parish system has been strained to its limits by modern conditions, but this has not irrevocably crippled Christianity, still less proved fatal to religion in general.

A second aspect of the secularization story, also related to the 'community-lost' thesis, is that older religious bases of morals and public authority are corroded in modern society. The next section, which covers some features of this, also highlights the ambiguities of this state of affairs. At a time of growing concern within the Churches about the exclusively temporal cast of current politics and administration, such ambiguities must be faced realistically. For it is possible that we have lost a common vocabulary within which to air such issues. And equally possible that attempts to 'reinstate' religious values in public life could in fact give birth to bastardized forms of Christianity.

From Public Morals to Parking Meters

'Hark, hark, the dogs do bark, the beggars are coming to town . . .' The words of this popular song, dating from Tudor times, is a reminder of the one-time local basis of justice and welfare. The dogs barked a warning of the arrival of beggars, a parish responsibility that many would have liked to evade. But each parish did have a duty to provide in some way for its impecunious citizens, and, especially under the later Victorian administration of the Poor Law, treatment was still meted out at this local level. Agreed codes, relating to the treatment of 'offenders' such as beggars, were not hard to find. Needless to say, in the days of the pioneer settlers of North America, similar systems of locally-agreed moral and judicial codes could be found.

Secularization studies frequently focus on the question of authority, morals and the legitimacy of government. A shift has occurred, it is said, from such locally-based moral consensus and administration of justice, to the impersonal, technical control of a scientific and bureaucratic age. In Wilson's words,

the large-scale societal community does not rely, or seeks not to rely, on a moral order, but rather, whenever possible, on a technical order . . . After all, if by time-and-motion studies, data retrieval systems, credit ratings, conveyor belts and electronic eyes, we can regulate men's activities, and in particular their vital economic functions, then why burden ourselves with the harrowing, arduous, time-consuming weariness of eliciting moral behaviour? (1982, p. 161)

Who then needs public morals, for instance to ensure the fair allocation of parking spaces, when the simple installation of meters will do the job? And at the wider level, if a simple technique cannot be found, then we can always legislate. Justice for minority groups in advanced societies is a case in point. If the idea of loving one's neighbour is at a low premium, then discrimination can be outlawed.

All this relates to a theme already touched on, that of the split between public and private social worlds engendered by industrial capitalism. As home and work, and work and leisure, were prised apart, so different moralities and different authorities came to govern the separated spheres. The public world was ruled by a new time discipline — clock-watching, the cash-nexus and the bureaucratic authority of 'experts'. The private world, on the other hand, became the realm — as far as personal means and circumstances allowed — of individual choice.

People in the advanced societies live 'administered' lives. From birth, when a plastic identity strip is immediately attached to the baby's wrist, to the death certificate which must accompany every passing from life, we are regulated and monitored. Even more so today when police national computers, department of health computers and credit card computers 'talk' to each other about our personal circumstances. The nation state as such is no longer particularly influenced by religious bodies (even in the USA). In capitalist contexts economies work with the dynamic of the profit motive, and even where state regulation is the order of the day, religion is not required within the economic 'mechanism'. The education system is not geared to any wider transcendental set of meanings, to wisdom, or to the unity of knowledge as an attribute of divine knowledge. Rather, as Bryan Turner has it, 'the administered society is characterized by a thick network of regulatory institutions which order and contain human activity' (Turner, 1983, p. 225). Little wonder, then, that people seek an escape from this kind of world in hedonistic mass consumerism—from spectator football to video rock-music—and the burgeoning market for private leisure activities.

The workplace exhibits many key traits of the administered society. Here the 'dull compulsion of economic life' is most evident. People labour for the pay packet, that is, 'instrumentally', and not for any intrinsic satisfaction which might be gained from their toil. Managers in particular are what Martin Goodridge calls 'secular practitioners' (1983). They are taught to pursue calculated ends, on a profit—loss basis, to maximize their self-interest, and to capitalize on every opportunity. The criteria on which they often operate might in another era have been condemned as avaricious, and contrary to the principle of stewardship. Today, this kind of attitude is not only encouraged at work, but it also spills over into the 'free time' activities of the manager. The buying of a house or the raising of children is carried out according to similar criteria.

What then has happened to religion as a legitimator of social and political order? Assumptions derived from conventional religious belief and practice certainly do not seem to have a high profile in today's bureaucracies and governments. The impersonal rules of office, law-court and laboratory are established without reference to Christian—or any other— morality. The powers-that-be seem to be legitimate in the public eye simply because of their duly established priorities, their effectiveness and their propriety. Some would also argue that in an age of increasing automation and robotization the need for controlling sanctions will be less, just because a lower proportion of the 'labour force' will in fact be required to 'labour'. One way or another, then, religion becomes redundant for the purposes of legitimation.

This position can be modified, however. Different circumstances do have different outcomes. For example, in the USA or Canada, where religion may be associated with some ethnic grouping, it may have more say in public legitimation. Other criteria than those of mere calculation and self-interest may be introduced, for example in 'civil rights'. Again, in some European countries, where there is still an established church, opportunities for a religious voice in the legitimation arena may not be entirely absent. At least at the critical level of questioning the credibility of government, the interventions of Anglican bishops in the British miners' strike of 1984, or of Polish priests who questioned the legality of secret police operations in 1985, do seem to have had some effect.

Another, more radical, difficulty faces those who wish to confront contemporary society with Christian codes of conduct. Do we all speak the same language? Alasdair MacIntyre avers that in the modern world we have actually lost the capacity to talk the language of morality and ethics. A far cry from the world in which religion was felt to be needed as a means of legitimation. In 1818, a Bill was before the English parliament to build more churches, thought necessary because of the 'vicious and corrupting influences dangerous to the public security as well as to private morality' (MacIntyre, 1967, p. 19). Andrew Ure, whose *Philosophy of Manufactures* influenced a generation of nineteenth-century entrepreneurs, viewed religion as a vital element in factory discipline.

During the nineteenth century, as class awareness and class-based antagonisms developed, new bases of social consensus were sought. MacIntyre suggests that a series of 'secondary virtues'—of co-operation, fair play, tolerance, and so on—emerged as the basis for social cohesion. This worked better, in Britain, than the attempts to found new religions (like Saint-Simon's) as an alternative to an older Christian ethic. The so-called Labour Churches, for example, failed to agree on how 'religious' they were: should they pray, or not, and if so, to whom? Thus it was, according to MacIntyre's interpretation, that public life retreated to the secondary virtues, gradually losing the ability to discuss issues in terms of 'primary virtues'. By the mid-twentieth century, he continues, this 'institutionalized confusion' was thoroughly embedded in school curricula. 'What our children are left with is on the one hand a vestigial Christian vocabulary of a muddled kind, and on the other an absence of any alternative vocabulary in which to raise the kinds of issues which it is necessary to raise if there is not to be a mere assessment of means about social and moral ends' (1967, p. 36).

Another angle on the diminishing social authority of religious language is provided by Richard Fenn, this time in a contemporary American context. He refers to authoritative religious utterance as 'liturgical language', because liturgy is the symbolic context for taking words seriously. However, he points out that the 'secularization of religious language' is proceeding apace in the modern world as the authority of the state, rather than religion, becomes the last court of appeal (1982). The state relies on rational and legal, not religious legitimation, the latter being thought of as essentially belonging to the 'private' sphere. This process is seen under a spotlight in the celebrated case of the death of Karen Ann Quinlan.

Quinlan, a young Catholic woman, had requested that her life never be maintained by entirely artificial means. But when controversy arose (and went to the courts) over whether or not her life-supporting machine be switched off, her 'liturgical' request was overruled by the evidence of medical 'experts'. Theirs was the language accepted by the courts. Her religion was reduced to personal opinion, her options restricted by the secularization of language. The court also assumed that the wider community would agree with this decision. Ironically, of course, the court accepts testimonies on oath, which, where a Bible is involved, must be seen as an appeal to religious authority. The point is that in fact the court—for the state—becomes the arbiter of what is and is not acceptable religious authority. Thus is the credibility and authority of religion diminished in modern society. It is simply made to count less.

Several of today's social analysts, well aware of the evacuation of religion from the public sphere, have alerted Western societies to a so-called crisis of legitimation (Habermas, 1976). Secularization has dissolved traditional forms of legitimation, and 'science' has been applied to politics. But this makes politics seem more remote from real life, so people slip into apathy and resignation, taking less and less seriously what technocratic politicians do and say. This is the root of the legitimation crisis.

Ideology took over as religion lost its hold as a legitimating force. But now modern ideologies are themselves implicitly rejected as failures (Gouldner, 1976). Secular thought-systems of the nineteenth century—liberalism, Marxism and so on—took the place of religious legitimation. But there are some significant differences between the two, says Gouldner. Both religion and ideology are used to control or at least influence behaviour. However, religion's main focus was everyday life, the immediate situation, whereas ideology relates to mobilized projects, to politics. Human beings are religiously seen as limited by finitude and sin (in the Christian account at least), but ideologically seen as having unlimited power and potential. An ideology makes 'what is' in society, rather than a revelation of what should be, the basis for action.

Here one can see clearly the drift away from any kind of religious basis for political life. Some, such as Habermas and Gouldner, see the problem as a lack of complete rationality. Others, such as Daniel Bell, believe that rationality itself is inadequate as a solution to the 'cultural contradictions of capitalism'. Classical liberalism and socialist utopianism indulged in *hubris,* he says, in thinking that the old could simply be cleared away in order to build anew (1976). Knowledge of power, the ideologists' dream, requires a knowledge of limits. Only religion can provide this, according to Bell.

Meanwhile, the supposed crisis of legitimation continues in Western societies (and also has its counterpart in Eastern Europe, as Poland especially illustrates). But there is one other source of legitimacy which, some say, retains its importance in the modern world. This is 'civil religion', a set of beliefs and rituals which relate to the past, present or future of a people (a 'nation'), and which is understood in a transcendent fashion. Most of the studies of this phenomenon originate in the USA, which is hardly surprising. Where Church and state have been traditionally separated for some time, one might expect some generalized form of legitimation to take shape.

Civil religion is said to be present in the American Declaration of Independence and in special national moments like presidential inaugural speeches. References are made to God as Creator and Judge, to Providence and Almighty Being—though 'controversial' allusions to Christ are omitted. This means that the civil religion can be made to appeal to a wide spectrum of people, including Jews, agnostics, Catholics as well as WASPs. Civil religion hints at parallels between America and the chosen people—Israel, and one even finds death, rebirth and sacrifice motifs in the Civil War and in the life and death of Abraham Lincoln.

Civil religion may well contribute to American social and political cohesion, but it is doubtful whether it could ever actually 'integrate' all sectors of American society ideologically. Pluralism, and the presence of dissenting minorities, are factors which cannot be ignored. At the same time, a question mark must be left hanging over whether religion or ideology *ever* held together any modern or modernizing society in a strong way. To a degree, Wilson is probably right. In so far as modern societies are kept together, it is by means of a complex web of bureaucratic regulations. Their dependence on goodwill, mutual trust and honesty is only implicit.

Religion on the Edge of Society

So where exactly is religion in the secular society? Part of the preparation of this book was done in Canada, where I looked in the *Kitchener—Waterloo Record* to find the answer. The Saturday edition carries ads for Sunday's services. I found I was invited to 'Worship in your car or bring a lawn chair' for 'Sunday evening in the park'. Muggy conditions could be overcome by another church's offer of 'worship in our air-conditoned sanctuary'. I was offered entertainment ('uplifting singing, exciting music'), and even the chance simply to stay at home and hear the evening service on CKGL FM 96.7. In other words, religion appeared in the newspaper as a leisure time alternative, something cut off from the public life of the weekday, and which could as well be 'received' in my armchair at home as anywhere else.

The third major theme in secularization studies is that of the marginalization of religion. The forces of modernity are said to push the realm of feeling, symbol and the spiritual to the edge of society. Religion is unwelcome at the centre of things (unless it can be appropriated for 'centre' purposes), and thus finds what remaining foothold it can at the periphery—in the private sphere. This is the realm *par excellence* of choice and of individual taste, of plural possibilities. Bryan Wilson again puts it neatly:

Religion becomes privatized. In a consumer society it becomes just another consumer good, a leisure-time commodity no longer affecting the centres of power or the operation of the system—even at the level of social control, socialization, and the organization of the emotions and of motivations. Religion becomes a matter of choice, but whatever religion is chosen is of no consequence to the operation of the social system (1976a, p. 277).

Here we see again the consequences of industrialism's splitting apart public and private worlds. Everyday life has been denuded of moral meaning, and reduced to repetitive routine. So the quest for meaning shifts into private and intimate areas of life. Family and sexuality are also seen as bestowing meaning, but all at the (commercialized) margin of society. This is one way in which the decline of 'Church-oriented religion' is described. Many social observers think that the degree of involvement in the work and processes of modern society relates directly to the degree of involvement in organized religion. The closer one is to the centre, the less one is likely to participate in religion of the conventional sort. The pattern may vary in different countries, classes, and with different types of religion, but the overall picture is accurate.

The USA does seem to be an exception to this pattern, as its rates of participation are proportionately higher than other Western societies. This is often explained in terms of the USA's different history (no feudal inheritance, official Church—state separation, the role of immigrant religions in providing social identities and cohesion and so on). But, it is said, this is only a surface phenomenon. A discernible 'internal secularization of the churches' shows that secularization is still the general American experience. Religion, which once contributed to the American Dream, is now pervaded *by* that dream. The churches, too, are socially uninfluential. The last part of the argument, it must be admitted, has been wearing thin since the end of the 1970s.

Two sociological questions are raised by the marginalization process. One, which has dominated discussion to the exclusion of the second, is how the process occurred. The other question is whether or not anything *replaces* religion in the modern world (Luckmann, 1967, p. 39). As to the first question, Luckmann is at pains to stress that neither industrialization, urbanism or even hostile science is the 'cause' of secularization. Rather, he says that the values of the Church were at one time more generally accepted as social norms. Industrialism and capitalism encouraged institutional specialization, thus cutting loose other institutions from the Church. So 'what were originally total life-values became part-time norms'. This is the reason for the marginalization of religion in the modern world—the uncoupling of Church and society.

At first glance, one might well imagine that the dissolving of tradition and the loss of a moral framework (for some at least), along with the routinizing of everyday life would produce something of a vacuum of meaning. Luckmann is not the only theorist to suggest that private areas of life would be the soil in which new social forms of religion would flourish. Both intimacy and sexuality on the one hand, and mass ritual, such as sport or nationalism on the other, have been offered as possible candidates.

Marginalization means that, apart from the state opening of parliament, and church weddings, religion is not a public affair. The term 'private' probably has something to do with English common-law usage. Into the Englishman's castle-home, 'the rain may enter, but the king cannot'. This is private space, supposedly insulated from the intrusions of the alien outside world. I say 'supposedly', because it is clear from examples already used that in fact the outside world does get in — through the TV screen, as work-styles spill over into leisure time, and as commercial pressures dictate how non-'work' time is spent. But as another example, that of Karen Ann Quinlan, shows, religion is publicly assumed to be only a private affair, of no public consequence.

As Peter Berger says, the Church, which once had some public clout, now has to compete to be heard at all. It becomes a marketing agency, as the Sunday service ads, sandwiched between the week's grocery bargains, display so well. Furthermore, all religions suffer from the lack of what Berger calls 'plausibility structures'. Existential choice, rather than socially accepted and supported belief, becomes the norm. The social climate is less conducive to shared faith. Religious 'options' proliferate to such an extent that one cannot but be 'heretical' to the next person (Berger, 1979). 'Orthodoxy' is an impossible category. As Weber said, each simply ends up following their personal 'demon'.

Private religion is a leisure-time pursuit. The British Central Statistical Office confirms this by placing religion next to camping, in the 'leisure' category! (Maybe they mean 'recreation'?) The churches often seem to accept this definition of their activities, becoming much like other voluntary organizations which offer certain services to the community. Little surprise, then, that in the summer time the beach and cottage can be such powerful counter-attractions. For leisure has to do with freedom from that which is necessary for existence. Peripheral to 'real' life, it is the sphere of relaxation, personal choice and pleasure.

What an irony! Religion has traditionally been a pretty serious business, especially when martyrdom is involved. Christian churches have always had an ambivalent attitude towards leisure. During the nineteenth century, as the churches had to compete for attention as one voluntary option among others, many did begin to use 'entertainment' as an attraction. The originally sober Methodist meetings had by the 1870s introduced more choirs, and organized their building interiors more for 'spectators'. In the USA, the music-hall style of Moody and Sankey became a legend. Even staid old Anglicans and Episcopalians began to indulge in new hymnody in order to keep up. Churchgoers could thus be excused for thinking that the churches had a leisure-time function.

Once, Sunday observance was a gauge of religiosity. Today's hedonism makes it a day for other pleasures and, increasingly, for commercialism. In fact, this is one of the few remaining areas for legislative controversy which involves church tradition. Should stores, banks and bars be open on Sunday? It raises the question of where is the boundary between sacred and secular worlds? And, will transgression lead to social hurt? It is assuredly another measure of the marginalization of religion when the voice of the churches is scarcely heard in the debate.

Bit by bit, then, it seems that organized religion is pushed to the edge of society. What are the social consequences of this? If the muting of religious values in the public realm, and their replacement by ideologies which are now found wanting, is at the back of legitimation crises, what might the privatizing of religion mean?

One significant impact is in the realm of identity—how people relate to society. Religion can no longer be expected to bestow stable social identities. The 'rites of passage', which help connect individual to society, persist, but often stripped of their original significance. In any case, as Berger says, one may be baptized a Catholic, marry a Jew, and be buried according to Protestant rites. Identities are more likely to be formed in private. In a world of passive consumers, Herbert Marcuse once warned, the formation of private identity is manipulated by the media, reducing us to a one-dimensional existence. Thus people seek new sources of stable identity — not least in religious, or quasi-religious ways. New religious movements, new 'Christian' gospels of 'self-esteem', and even psychology (see Vitz, 1977) betray signs of this quest.

The other significant area of impact is within the Christian fold. Here the identity question has a further twist to it. With religion increasingly isolated on the 'private' side of the public/private split of modern life, the public identity of Christians tends to be weak. No one expects Christians to pass comment, or influence decisions as *Christians,* on the underdevelopment of the Southern hemisphere, nuclear weapons, the uses made of company profits, how the city council treats its minorities or what the school includes in its curriculum. The current enthusiasms for home-based church groups, Christian entertainment on TV and cassette, and for private sphere preoccupations such as 'how-to' manuals for family life tend — whatever their intrinsic merits — to reinforce this trend.

Little wonder that the secularization story is usually recounted in gloomy tones as each bleak chapter unfolds. After all the image — and all-too-often the reality — is that of religion which is generally assumed to have little relevance to real life, and which is carefully domesticated at home as a harmless pastime for those maladjusted to modernity.

For society at large, one has to agree that a general 'secularization of consciousness' is occurring, at least in so far as this involves a diminishing public recognition that God might have anything to do with current human affairs. For secularization is about more than 'community-lost', or the marginalizing of religion. The subjective side to this is that people appeal less to the supernatural or to God for explanation or aid. Durkheim was right to foresee the continued rise in public acceptance of what is loosely called 'humanism', whose interests are firmly fixed to the *saeculum* — this temporal, passing age. The Church is not immune from this either. Today's obsessions with the 'ethic of love' and social justice may actually divert attention from, rather than demonstrate the relevance of, the God 'out there'.

That said, the secularization story must still be qualified. Massive variations exist, as we shall see. Also, the story tends to focus, in a reductionist manner, on those social aspects of religion which are either historical accretions (religion as entertainment) or unintended consequences (religion as political legitimator), rather than expressions of the essence of Christian faith and practice. If Christianity was not primarily designed to act as social glue—as Wilson seems to think it was—then the fact that society may come 'unstuck' does not mean Christianity has been deprived of its pristine power.

4: The Varieties of Secular Experience

Secularization seems to be a universal experience of the industrialized societies. Similar effects may be traced from Saskatchewan to Singapore. But it is not the blind, relentless and uniform force that some would have us believe. Without evading the crucial issue of what is actually happening to society and Christianity in secularizing societies, it is vital to get a feel for the nuances of secularization in different settings and circumstances.

The varieties of secular experience discussed in this chapter include differences made by the relationship between Church and state, what social class or which generation one belongs to, and so on. So we are examining the splitting apart of society and religion in different contexts. The point is to raise awareness of the form secularization takes in specific situations, and also to see how these varieties lead us to question the old-fashioned 'blanket' views of secularization.

The inheritors of the classical tradition of social theory imagined that secularization was a one-way street, with no 'U-turns' allowed. The modern condition militated against the survival of any form of religion. The Church had lost its position of social dominance and influence; 'irrationality' had no home in the rational society. With the pioneer sociologists as our guide, as Donald MacRae has put it, 'we should expect disenchantment to become complete, bureaucracy and regulation universal, and secularization to displace all the meaning of faith and hope while administrative welfare eliminates charity' (MacRae 1974, p. 87).

The secularization story does leave this impression. Belief is more difficult in the modern world, so it is said, and the churches have to cope with a less congenial climate, if not outright hostility. Mobility has eroded older face-to-face relationships, and the split between public and private social worlds has left religion stranded on the inconsequential 'private' side. Metaphysical homelessness is the modern condition. And society does not need religion.

But is it such a one-way street? Is the secularization process so directly and necessarily caused by becoming modern? And does it really steamroller the spirit in this way? Such notions derive more from the assumptions which form the warp of nineteenth-century social thinking on which the received secularization design is woven. So while it is of utmost importance to understand why secularization has occurred, and what it entails for social life in contemporary society, these assumptions must be questioned. This chapter shows how the 'strong' secularization story finds its main strength in simplicity. The more accurate picture is one of immense complexity, ambiguity and paradox. There is a variety of secular experience. So much so, that the secularization story is found wanting as a conceptual lens for scrutinizing our social surroundings. The strength of the secularization story is its weakness.

Differences of Time and Place

'Things are not equal—ever—' says David Martin, with respect to secularization, 'and . . . they are most conspicuously not equal with respect to the particular cultural (and general linguistic) complex within which they operate' (Martin, 1978, p. 3). The general tendencies of secularization are squeezed through what Martin calls 'historical filters', which alter markedly the patterns of secularization observable in different countries. Martin Marty, of the University of Chicago, was one of the first to document the influence of these 'historical filters'. In *The Modern Schism,* he makes visible the varieties of secularization, at least at the 'history of ideas' level. He describes three situations: the 'utter secularity' of France, the 'mere secularity' of England, and the 'controlled secularity' of the USA.

In France, the attempt to render the world utterly secular involved 'devastating and then replacing Christendom'. The frontal attack during the eighteenth-century Enlightenment is remembered by the cry 'crush the infamous thing' (the Church), and by numerous schemes for rebuilding society without recourse to Christian symbols. The universal system of education for example, set up in Napoleonic times, was designed to take the place of any training previously the province of the Church. 'A clerical society', Marty observes, 'bred anticlericalism'. Later in the nineteenth century, the cry turned to 'God is dead!', as people declared that Christianity meant *bad* faith, enslavement and error. This is the continental form of the 'modern schism' — a clear split between old world and new. What happened in other *milieux* was rather different.

Things in England were a lot less apocalyptic than in France. French influence was feared politically, and the fact that atheism was conjoined with revolutionary Jacobinism meant that French ideas had little serious impact (except negative impact) in England until the last quarter of the nineteenth century. To quote Marty,

England knew a few minor god-killers and now and then provided a home for continental ideas or advocates of ideas about the deaths of God, Church, and Christian culture. But twentieth-century heirs of the legacy of those ideas do not have to deal seriously with the thought about the death of God in England. Rather, they have to reckon with people who began to ignore Christian claims, to become impervious to them; people who found that God, Church, and Christian teaching were superfluous to their thought and action. (Marty, 1967, p. 19)

Hence Marty's designation of the English context as 'mere secularity'. In contrast with the swashbuckling secularizing policy of the French, the English experience is somewhat drab and bland. Undoubtedly, though, for those who passed through the years of 'doubt' and the Victorian 'loss of faith', it was nonetheless a painful and anxious time.

God-killers and atheists were even more rare in the USA. However, Marty is convinced that a 'drastic religious change' occurred in the mid-nineteenth-century decades. Industrialization and urbanization were already in motion, and an 'autonomous culture' — that is, free from any explicit religious commitment — was emerging. 'Yet', says Marty, 'it was screened from view in part because of religious leaders' ability to disguise the secularizing change by adapting and reapplying symbols of Christian reminiscence and continuity at significant points of change' (1967, p. 20).

What he means is this. America's religious leaders so controlled the symbols of religion as they related to social and personal life, that radical change could occur without disrupting the continuity of those symbols. Salvation language would still be used, but while the earlier clergy might be thinking primarily of the *after life,* later clergy would in fact have *this life* in mind. According to early-nineteenth-century sermons, the poor were to be content, the affluent stewardly and charitable; things would be evened out later. But by the late nineteenth century the poor were told to aspire to escape their status for middle-class rewards. The middle class, on the other hand, should scorn the poor, whose indolence kept them from sharing their position. The 'social gospel', which made its début towards the *fin de siècle,* also transformed the kingdom of God motif into an almost exclusively *this-worldly* concern. Theocratic symbols, which made America appear as the new Israel, also changed. As Lincoln reminded the new nationalists on both sides of the Civil War, they were no longer prepared to see themselves as being under God. Rather, the nation, with its 'manifest destiny', seemed itself to take the place of God.

Thus historic spiritual concerns were still addressed during the transition to scientific and industrial culture. Institutional religion was in fact greatly expanded. But according to Marty what happened was that religious forces accepted a novel division of labour. They were boxed in. 'In the new social contract, religion acquiesced in the assignment to address itself to the personal, the familial, and leisured sectors of life while the public dimensions—political, social, economic, cultural—were to become autonomous or to pass under the control of other kinds of tutelage' (1967, p. 98). This, of course, is what we have referred to as marginalization and privatization.

It is worth pausing to note a sub-theme which recurs throughout Marty's analysis. He entitled his work *The Modern Schism* in order to 'indicate that secularization did not mean the disappearance of religion so much as its relocation' (1967, p. 11). For example, not only the Americans of manifest destiny, but British imperialists and French and Italian nationalists 'tended to make a god of the state and then to invoke reminiscence of Christianity to justify their creation' (1967, p. 57). Marty thus hints strongly at the answer to the 'other' secularization question which, as Luckmann regrets, has been so widely ignored. That is, what replacement, if any, was sought in the face of the demise of Christendom? In Britain, Marty implies, it was not only political, but also scientific deities which caught the imagination and devotion of at least some intellectuals. More generally, Marty says, the industrial ethos and the urban drift together demanded as comprehensive an interpretation of life as had previously been offered by Christianity. Both secular dogmas *and* everyday practices showed how far North Atlantic nations were moving beyond Christendom. Marty thus displays a common trend within these varieties of secularization, towards 'this-worldly' or *temporal* concerns. Accompanying this is a tendency to try to find quasi-religious alternatives to the visibly shrinking Christendom.

This theme, the shrinking of Christendom, also forms the backdrop to David Martin's *A General Theory of Secularization*, which is a landmark in secularization studies. In a more sociological, and more theoretically sophisticated fashion than Marty, he analyses the varieties of secularization in many different contexts. His stress is on the growing apart of Church and state, or what we have referred to as the 'uncoupling' of their institutions. But while to do so he draws on political sociology, it is from economics that he borrows his most important ideas! As he says, 'The right sociological question is already nearly the right answer, and I believe that the fundamental question is the beginning and progress of religious *laissez-faire*' (Martin 1979, p. 1).

By 'religious *laissez-faire*' Martin means the loosening of Church—state bonds. That is, 'free market' religion, where no one is under any obligation to believe anything at all, where one's religious creed does not prejudice one's attaining political office, and where no agreement with religious articles is required for educational opportunity. In such a *laissez-faire* situation, one might anticipate that a luxuriant variety of religious plants would flourish.

The opposite of *laissez-faire* is, of course, monopoly. And Christendom was the greatest religious monopoly ever. The splitting of Christendom's sacred canopy by the Reformation meant the genesis of numerous patterns of secularization. In some cases Catholicism reasserted itself, tightening the monopoly, but monarchs frequently took control themselves, thus co-opting the Church to the state's ends (Peter the Great and Henry the Eighth are two examples). In other cases, Church and state disentangled themselves, becoming separate but equal powers. America's Puritans are a case in point. One need not necessarily have extremes, either. In England Charles the Second renationalized the church in 1660, but allowed dissent, or 'nonconformity' to grow as well.

Already the contours of Martin's theory must be seen in fairly clear relief. France is an instance of the monopoly situation, America of *laissez-faire*, or 'free market' religion, and England of a 'mixed economy'. Another category is 'duopoly', where two churches exist in the same country, as in the Netherlands or Northern Ireland. In this case the likelihood is that the smaller church becomes involved in reformist politics, but religious differences are not themselves a source of conflict. (Unless, that is, as in Northern Ireland, a majority of co-religionists is just a bomb's throw away, across the border. Religion and political identity then get fatally mixed.)

Martin's theory gives some essential illuminative clues as to why secularization occurs in one way here and another way there. He shows how the previous religious situation has a close bearing on the eventual secular outcome. Not that a religious monopoly, as in Russia, *causes* the emergence of a secular monopoly (of dogmatic, conservative Marxist-Leninism which cannot allow *any* religion to blossom) but rather that there are 'suggestive connections' between the two. It is what sociologists call an 'explanatory variable'. And it helps explain in particular the political organization of modern societies, and their connection, if any, with conventional religion. In the monopoly, religion is linked up with the fortunes of the state, so if the old order is blasted, then the established church is blasted along with it. Which throws light on the strength of anti-clericalism in France. In the *laissez-faire*, or pluralist situation, religion as such is not an important issue, so a plethora of denominations and sects are free to develop (as is a non-established secular*ism* — think, for example, of the founding of Cornell University in New York State as a secular response to the many American *religious* university foundations). In the mixed situation — England, Canada or Australia — a minority church may often be seen to contribute to the stabilizing of the political sphere by appearing on the centre-left. British liberals, with their non-conformist roots, are an obvious example.

Martin's general theory also shows why 'secularization' is a concept best applied in the Western, post-Christendom context. For it is in this context that the unique experiment to disconnect political authority and religious faith occurred. He goes on,

That disconnection is actually implied in the Christian religion itself. Which is why it happened in Christian society and not elsewhere and why Christianity digs at its own foundations. The separation of Caesar and God, nation and religion is paradoxically the end of religion, but the essence of Christianity. (1979, p. 12)

Martin's mood is certainly not one of unmitigated gloom over the secularization patterns which he has so skilfully uncovered. The 'essence of Christianity', as he sees it, cannot be mortally wounded by the collapse of Christendom, or by the failure of any temporary political alliances on which the Church may from time to time embark. His theory of secularization patterns is an antidote to the inevitability and uniformity which has often infected secularization studies.

Differences of Class, Culture and Generation
Why are Western Christian churches so frequently derided as being bastions of middle-class culture? Why was the British Anglican Church once lampooned as the 'Tory party at prayer' (or now, as the Social Democratic Party at prayer)? Why the widespread fear that the 'younger generation' have rejected the religion of their parents? Do these common feelings not suggest that, even if modern societies are in some significant sense 'secular', that secularity is rather unevenly distributed within the population?

One of the most common exaggerations in the received secularization story is manifest in phrases like 'the rationalization of society'. This gives the impression that society is affected *as a whole* by some form of secularization. Just as talk of a Christian society existing in medieval Europe is misleading, because different sectors of the population varied in their opinion of and adherence to the Church, so it also misleads to speak of a 'secular society'. Secularity is found at different levels of intensity within the various classes, cultures and generations which make up any given society. Moreover, things are seldom stable. Movements of religion *and* secularity are usually discernible at any point in history—at the same time and in the same place. In their turn, such movements may help foster a social climate more or less congenial to the spread of Christian, or other, religion.

In order to put secularization in proper perspective, to give the concept further clarity and accuracy, the groups, classes and movements which 'carry' secularization must be examined. Of course, this once again involves placing the whole debate in a comparative and historical context. This can be done by considering three questions which are often high on the agenda for church discussion. Firstly, the gap between the so-called working classes and the churches, secondly, the related suspicion that religion is the province of dominant social élites, and thirdly, the feeling that secularization (in the sense of a publicly-accepted belief that religion is irrelevant today) may be accelerated by conflict between generations.

Pope Pius XI is supposed to have said that 'The greatest scandal of the Church in the nineteenth century was that it lost the working class.' Bishop Winnington-Ingram of London commented, just before his enthronement in 1901, 'it is not that the Church of God has lost the great towns: it has never had them' (quoted in McLeod, 1980, p. 191). The truth, of course, probably lies somewhere between the two positions. The 'great towns' of Europe did evidence lower church attendance relative to rural areas during the nineteenth century.

In the famous English religious census of 1851 only 36 per cent of the population were in church at all. Its co-ordinator, Horace Mann, took this as a sign of the 'spiritual destitution' of the large towns. But in fact *within* the large towns there was a considerable variation. Despite the fact that Christianity was supposed to have become a 'middle-class religion' in Victorian Britain, until about 1850 (from 1780) the Protestant dissenting denominations such as Congregationalists, Baptists, Calvinistic and Arminian Methodists enjoyed 'spectacular growth' (McLeod, 1980, p. 205). Many of these, as we have already observed, were 'working-class' people. In fact, in the second half of the nineteenth century there were more working-class than middle-class churchgoers in many areas for much of the time. Moreover, upper-class participation was also greater than middle-class.

Jeffrey Cox's study of the London Borough of Lambeth (1870—1930) throws light where others, stuck with a simplistic secularization concept, have misled us (1982). Although Lambeth cannot be representative in detail for other areas, certain features of its church life do apply fairly broadly. Cox shows that while upper- and middle-class church attendance grew in his period, this does not mean that the working class was simply 'alienated' from organized religion.

While E. R. Wickham's conclusion, based on an examination of the Yorkshire city of Sheffield, is that some churches failed to accommodate themselves to new urban populations (Wickham, 1957), and thus effectively excluded newcomers, Cox insists that in fact the churches did keep in touch with the working class. They may not have persuaded them to come to church, but their vast network of 'welfare' and philanthropic activity successfully kept them in the gravitational field of the churches. Only when other institutions arose to put such activities on a more rationally organized footing did they lose this contact. That said, what members of the 'working class' believed is another question. Cox devotes considerable attention to what he found quite extensively in South London: 'diffusive Christianity'. This contained nothing 'intensely supernatural', but a veneration of 'Christian ethics', plus a God 'borrowed from Christianity' and a fair dose of fatalism, luck, rites of passage and respectability (1982, chapter 4).

Of course, cultural communication gaps existed between middle and working class. But it was also a difference of practice: voluntary associations were generally more popular among the middle classes. For the latter, religion was often a matter of social propriety. And of course some working-class people suffered a 'loss of faith', though this was more because of moral objections or the apparently greater relevance of political activity than because of secular*ism* (see Budd, 1979, pp. 122–3). In this the French situation is something of a contrast. Ironically, although local community persisted longer in working-class *milieux* (often associated with a dominant occupation), religious adherence was not necessarily maintained (Gilbert, 1980, pp. 86–91).

American religion is also class-linked. Protestantism in particular has persistently fulfilled a role within the class system, as a vehicle of social mobility and class symbolism. Berger comments on the class effect on affiliation:

From the cool upper-class regions of certain Episcopalian or Unitarian parishes, through the broadly bourgeois zones of

Methodist or Baptist congregations, to the somewhat sweaty 'upper-lower-class' (to use Lloyd Warner's slightly dated term) gathered in Pentecostal or Holiness assemblies . . . The progress of secularization too has had its class indices all along, carrying much more momentum in the upper as against the lower reaches of the system. (Berger, 1983)

The class dimension of secularization is one which has been glossed in many accounts. But it is misleading to think of secularization only in relation to national societies. This helps makes sense of the differences between Martin and Wilson. Wilson sees the Church as steadily withering from its one-time position of social dominance, because of urbanism, differentiation and modernization. Martin on the other hand says that because the Church *never* successfully incorporated the 'incorrigible peasantry' (because its cultural control was largely confined to cities), the idea of 'church dominance' is inaccurate. In a sense, as Bryan Turner has noted, both are right. For the dominant classes in Europe, religion often did have an essential function in organizing social behaviour. But at the same time, the mass of the peasantry *was* largely excluded from the religious position of the dominant class (Turner, 1983, pp. 142–6).

Class position does make a difference to the way secularization occurs, and this means that any simple story must be distrusted. Many nineteenth-century secularists were intellectuals, who wanted to form a new non-theological 'clerisy' (the term is Coleridge's) to replace the priesthood. In the USA, this is echoed in Marty's 'autonomous culture' of secularism. On both sides of the Atlantic, this group attempted to control the media of opinion by such expedients as obtaining journal editorships. This had a definite effect on the course of secularization itself. For those secularists, who pressed for instance for education to be a state, not a Church concern, actually contributed by such actions to the uncoupling of Church and state.

The class question has a further twist to it today. It is one thing to focus on the alleged and often all-too-real working-class disaffection from organized Christianity, another to ponder the fortunes of the middle classes. Since the Second World War, the old middle class has shown signs of splitting. The old *bourgeoisie,* with its commercial and professional cadres, is on one side. On the other side is a social stratum deriving its livelihood from writing, filming, recording, broadcasting and so on—what is called 'the production and distribution of symbolic knowledge'. These are not just 'intellectuals', but a range of communications people, therapists, bureaucrats and others of their ilk. Peter Berger in particular has put forward the argument that secularity is firmly established in this latter class, or quasi-class (1983).

Alvin Gouldner also offers a version of the 'knowledge class' idea. For him, its emergence was bound up with European secularization. As the Church came to be less involved in the training of intellectuals, so authority became 'desacralized'. People could define social (and other) reality in a more independent manner. Gouldner holds that this relatively unsupervised 'New Class' is an increasingly influential 'cultural *bourgeoisie*' (1979).

Following Berger, sociologists of religion show how present American cultural conflicts make sense in terms of the struggle for power and privilege between the divided halves of the old *bourgeoisie*. Their choice of cultural symbols is not accidental. It includes abortion, the Equal Rights Amendment (ERA), gay rights, environmental protection and so on. The implication is that secularity appears on the New Class side, and thus the religious/secular boundary question is thrust more and more into the political sphere. The New Class, it is said, prefer to see things only in a temporal dimension, and resist or discount any attempts to locate contemporary questions within a religious perspective. It would certainly appear that the contest is seen this way by the religious protagonists. As one sharply focused statement has it: 'Most of the evils of our day can be traced to Humanism . . . It is destroying our culture, families, country . . . Humanism is the godless, groundless secular religion which underlies the warped and dangerous thinking behind much of the social activism of our time. It is satanic in origin . . .' (quoted in Hunter, 1983, p. 110).

It remains to be seen just how accurate is this analysis of the religious-cultural conflicts of today. For one thing, it is plain that many members of the 'cultural *bourgeoisie*' are the very evangelicals whose blistering critique has just been quoted. They, whose publishing houses and TV programmes are booming, can hardly be excluded from the ranks of the symbolic knowledge handlers. For another, while one doubts that *all* members of the New Class are consciously conspiring to accelerate the secularization of Western society, within it, pressure groups of various sorts do exist. Just as some members of the Christian 'New Right' hark back to the 'New Israel' idea in the USA, humanist members of the New Class strive entirely to erase religion from the human agenda.

One other factor which deserves mention at this point is generation. At a common sense level, the history of religion and society might lead one to expect generational conflict over matters of religion and morals. Surprisingly enough, not much work has been done on this. An exception is a pioneer study done by Robert Wuthnow on the part played by generation in post-1960s cultural conflicts. Applying Karl Mannheim's concept of a 'generational unit' to the 'counter-culture' of the 1960s, Wuthnow draws attention to cultural and religious cleavage between different age-groups. He suggests that the relative fall-off in church activity since the 1960s may in part be attributable to the existence of a 'counter-culture'. A self-conscious generational group with its own symbols may have deflected attention from and adherence to the traditional churches in the USA. Members had commitments of their own (of both a religious and a temporal kind) which meant that they did not show up on the sociologists' usual indicators of religious involvement.

If this is correct, then it has further implications for the tale of secularization. The long-term, evolutionary approach, which labours the connection of secularization with industrialism, urbanism or modernization, cannot cope with hiccups in the data, such as those presented by the 1970s in the USA. But introduce the idea of generational differences, and one has a plausible explanation of the fall-off in conventional religious involvement. This in turn means that long-term predictions about secularization may be quite misplaced. As Wuthnow says, if current trends are 'the product of a specific generation unit, they may be of indeterminate duration. As successive age-strata mature, not having experienced the counter-cultural contagion of the 1960s, there may well be a return to the more conventional religious commitments; indeed, there already has been some evidence to this effect' (Wuthnow, 1976, p. 862).

So secularization need not be thought of as a monolithic

process, the inescapable consequence of becoming modern. Some societies are more likely to be secular than others—in the sense of deliberately cutting themselves loose from expressions and institutions of conventional religion—but there are also important differences of secular experience which depend on one's class, cultural or generational situation. Each context must therefore be examined for its unique aspects. Moreover, alternative possibilities and directions must also be expected.

From the viewpoint of the Christian churches, all this means that little headway will be made without *appropriate* responses to modern circumstances. One need not underestimate the power of prayer or the reality of the Spirit to see the sense in a realistic appraisal of opportunities and obstacles. A couple of examples may help. Churches attempting to 'build bridges' to 'working-class' culture do well to remember that they are likely to encounter updated versions of pre-Christian superstition and folk belief among this stratum (at least in many European societies). On the other hand, those constructing dykes against 'New Class' secular*ism,* or trying to make inroads into their communications-media territory, must expect a more 'post-Christian' outlook to be prominent. As ever, though, the flow of attitudes and practices can become two-way. False alliances start subtly. One may already discern the diverting impact of Marxism among some of today's 'urban missionaries', or of a thinly-veneered materialism among some Christian entertainment incomers.

This chapter has focused more on the social responses to the 'uncoupling' of religious from other institutions, and on the degrees of distance between conventional religion and social activity at various levels. The next chapter is also about anomalies and variations in the secularization story, although the focus now shifts more to the 'rationalization' side of the story.

5: Unsecular Society

Modern science and technology are in many ways the main carriers of the secular outlook. The spirit of rational calculation, typical of science and technology, has invaded the world of commerce, politics, education and even some areas of private life as well. As Peter Berger says, we have created a 'world without windows', ironically shutting out the light of life-sustaining wisdom. Today, our new information technologies threaten to take the same process further, faster. The implications of this are tremendous.

This chapter examines some of the questions surrounding this 'rationalization' of society. While the world's windows are still kept firmly closed against light from beyond, the signs are that rationalization is far from complete. Many scientists are deeply religious. Technology easily becomes an idol. And in wider society, outbursts of new religious activity (Christian and other), and the persistence of age-old ritual belief and practice, cast doubt on whether society *can* ever become fully rationalized.

The challenge for sociology, then, is to accept what its pioneers intuitively felt: that some kind of religion is bound up with the very constitution of society. This dimension is omitted from analysis at our peril. The challenge for Christianity is to recognize not only the ways in which society, and the churches, may succumb to secularity, but also to discover the specific directions in which quasi-religious allegiance has now turned.

The classic secularization journey leads, by various routes, to a single destination; secular society. In this land, the erstwhile public role of religion is hugely diminished. It will be clear by now, however, that the classic journey is one that has both been embellished by travellers' tales and reduced to the commercial simplicity of a travel agent's catalogue. We have discovered in fact that the trip varies, depending on the specific context. Just as rural scenery or concrete cityscape take on quite different characteristics depending on season, so secularization looks different when filtered through nation, class, culture or generation. And rather like the traveller, disappointed by failed expectation, the careful analyst of secularization eventually realizes that 'secular society' is not necessarily what lies at the end of secularization studies.

Let me say quickly that I am not for a moment denying that the modern world has thrown up some novel social configurations which have affected the contours of religious commitment in the late twentieth century. Nor am I saying that the secularization story is sheer fabrication, or that religion lives on, unchanged and unscathed by 'modernity'. Indeed, both social institutions, such as education and the law, and the churches themselves, cannot hope to operate successfully in the 1980s and 1990s without coming to terms with the impact of both the uncoupling of Church and society, and the culture of calculation with its 'disenchanting' tendencies. Having said that, though, the fact remains that 'secular society' is still not bound to be the end of the road. Perhaps we ought rather to speak of 'unsecular society'.

The grim logic of Max Weber's 'rationalization' hypothesis is that one day all vestiges of spirituality, symbolism and ritual would be wiped out. True, he did not utterly discount the possibility that new 'charismatic' figures might arise, or that 'prophecy' could challenge the juggernaut of the calculative mentality. But he counselled that we assume the contrary, and simply beaver away at the tasks of the present, without assistance or direction from 'outside' sources.

However, Weber did not take his own theory seriously enough. He saw the category of 'calculating rational action' as just one of four possible types of 'rationality'. The others include rational action based on tradition, or that based on certain transcendent goals or values. Yet these two types of rational action, when embodied in religious commitment, have frequently been discounted (even in Weber's own writing) as 'irrational'. It is true that within a bureaucracy, for example, the internal rules (calculative rationality) may swallow up any goal-based rationality. The procedures become paramount. But the calculative approach is not guaranteed victory. Indeed, we now turn to some evidence that the merely calculative approach is in some trouble in the last part of the twentieth century. Perhaps humans have an inbuilt resistance to life which has been shrunk to the level of calculation only. Maybe not only Christianity but also secularity digs its own grave. As Leszek Kolakowski points out, it is only a matter of time before those who announced that no conclusive proof exists of religious reality, will be forced to recognize that the same applies to 'secular reality' (1982, p. 97).

The evidence before us has to do in the first place with science and technology, as obvious carriers of the calculative mentality. Science, in Victorian times at least, was often thought to be displacing Christian belief. Since the Second World War, hopes have been pinned on 'technology' to guarantee the future. In the present, 'information technology', that recent marriage of computing and telecommunications, would appear to be the acme of electronic rationality. Will it finish the task begun by science last century?

The second type of evidence we examine below seems to fly in the face of any hypothetical 'disenchantment' which may have overtaken Western society. It is the revival, resurgence, return or at the very least the persistence of religious movements in the modern world. Looking at these, however, we find that the evidence is not unambiguous. The new forms that religion is taking raise once more the question of the definition of religion.

Science, Technology, and the Death of God

Peter Berger once argued that the development of science was crucial to 'opening the floodgates of secularization'. Protestantism, having 'cut the umbilical cord between heaven and earth' by reducing communication to a single line of 'God's word', then courted final disaster by clearing the way for modern science and technology. For science plucked away the plausibility of the 'word'. The rest is easy. 'A sky empty of angels, becomes open to the intervention of the astronomer and, eventually, the astronaut' (1969, p. 112).

Today, however, the complacent assumption that science deals a death-blow to all forms of belief in God, and even to God himself, is increasingly difficult to maintain. This is a cause for concern among those who fear that God could still be alive. One 'alarmed friend of the scientific outlook' for instance, perceives a 'sea of opposition surging against scientific methodology' in contemporary America. He goes on,

The metaphoric waters I refer to are composed of credulity,

gullibility, and high-energy ignorance and are manifested pre-eminently in three psycho-social phenomena. The first is old-time religion—something that educated people, both believers and non-believers, had thought was safely behind us in the old times, where it belongs. But alas modern, scientific, progressive America is witnessing a reactivation of biblical literalism, fundamentalism, and evangelicalism that almost defies belief . . . it spells trouble for science, reason, intelligence, and the free mind (McKown, 1981, p. 336).

Of course, other friends of the scientific outlook are equally worried by myopia and anti-intellectual fanaticism which are exhibited by some forms of religion. But the writer of these words, in seeing religion and science as implacable enemies, fails both to make some important distinctions (for instance between fundamentalism and evangelicalism), and to note some rather interesting connections—even symbiosis—between religion and science.

Popular opinion (including popular sociology or psychology!) has from time to time equated science with unbelief. This is the cultural myth that religion and science cannot mix. However, this mood has been changing for some time, and what has begun as a reappraisal of relationships within the scientific establishment could eventually percolate into other social layers.

An examination of the actual attitudes of scientists shows in fact that science does not displace religious commitment. This is especially true where natural scientists are concerned—scholars in the social sciences and humanities may be somewhat less religiously committed (Hoge and Keeter, 1976, p. 234). Indeed Albert Einstein himself asserted that 'the cosmic religious experience is the strongest and noblest driving force behind scientific research' (quoted in Lemert, 1979, p. 445). And even if the majority of scientists are not formally committed to some recognizable religious option, they do exhibit an open-mindedness about religion which would instil despair in our 'scientific outlook' friend.

Now, this kind of evidence could simply be set directly against the crude rationalization thesis and used as an argument for 'unsecular society'. Another approach is to ask 'what might be done to explain the fact that no one has yet proven definitively that science secularizes scientists and that perhaps as many as sixty-three per cent of even the hardest of hard scientists (in the USA) still look favourably on religion'? (Lemert, 1979, p. 447) Lemert, drawing on the sociology of science, proposes that in fact science in the present may be viewed as a sort of substitute for religion. More precisely, Lemert is suggesting that *scientism,* as a popular attitude of uncritical 'respect' for, or 'belief' in things scientific, could be a new 'sacralized ideology' (1979, p. 455). It may be used to legitimate aspects of both public policy and private lifestyle. 'Put a white laboratory jacket on an actor and toothpaste will sell. Claim that exploration of the moon is necessary to maintain the United States' "scientific superiority" and the Congress will support the NASA budget'.

Lemert's conclusion is that any simplistic equation of science with secularity is false. Many scientists are such precisely because of their religious commitment; many others seem to treat science in a way not entirely distinguishable from religion. He recalls Heisenberg's doubt that 'human societies can live with a sharp distinction between knowledge and faith' (1979, p. 459), and suggests that the existence of 'scientism' makes good sociological sense of Heisenberg. Of course, from a Judeo-Christian viewpoint, scientism is secular in the sense that it takes the place of religion as providing the world-view context for science. But 'viewed sociologically, with reference to their structural place in technocratic societies, scientism and the rationalized scientific conscious-ness are not necessarily very secular at all' (1979, p. 460).

However, discussing science before technology may be construed as putting the cart before the horse. Historically, technology has developed first, in response to a practical problem, be it the slowness of a handloom or the military requirement to crack enemy codes. Scientific research follows. Mining gives rise to geology, sea-navigation to astronomy. But the popular perception of science and technology places them the other way round. Science is often seen more immediately for its putative secularizing tendencies. However, the reminder that technology is always developed to meet some felt need at once exposes the secularizing potential of technology.

French sociologist Simondon expresses this potential thus:

By reducing the object to nothing but its dimensions, technology does not recognize in it any internal or symbolic meaning or any significance beyond its purely functional utility . . . the object is sufficient in itself and is not the carrier of intentions . . . 'technology desacralizes the world' to the extent that it successively imprisons man in nothing but objects without allowing him to catch a glimpse of a higher reality (quoted in Acquaviva, 1979, p. 140).

Technology is here seen in a negative light, as the bearer of a constricting consciousness. There are at least two aspects to this.

Arnold Gehlen has shown how on the one hand the technological outlook corrodes old certainties by giving the impression that everything is manipulable, inherently changeable. Humans have an apparently infinite power to shape their environment. Ethical constraints have gone, only technical ones remain, and they are always provisional (1980, p. 101). Not only is the sky open to the astronomer and astronaut, space colonies will soon welcome their first settlers. The existence of chronic hunger on planet earth puts no moral brakes on the space programme. Humanistic *hubris* comes home to roost.

On the other hand, Gehlen sees technological society inducing an inward turn, as people seek meaning in the world from which it has been drained. Spurning the ethic of God-and-neighbour love, they are (to quote Tocqueville) 'constantly circling round in pursuit of the petty and banal pleasures with which they glut their souls. Each one of them, withdrawn into himself, is almost unaware of the fate of the rest' (1980, p. 97). This 'secular horizon', artificially set by technology, paradoxically limits our vision by depriving the world both of a sense of God's presence, and of his claims on human responsibility.

Bryan Wilson concurs with this, at least in so far as technology seems to take morality out of social control: 'electronic eyes and data retrieval systems have largely supplanted interpersonal concern and the deeply implanted virtues of honesty, industry, goodwill, responsibility and so on' (1982, p. 42). Morality rooted in religion is rendered obsolete. As anti-theft devices prevent our leaving the library with unchecked books, and electronic eyes monitor traffic control systems, we find rational operations taking over each sector of life.

But this time Wilson seems a little uncertain of himself. He notes some possible limits to this technological secularization. For one thing, human technical competence could be a source of problems, 'since we tend to have faith in new techniques even though there are issues of life which technology cannot resolve' (1982, p. 42). For another, Wilson sees signs of some disillusion with new technologies, which seem 'rationally' to destroy the environment or the physical base of community. Nevertheless, he warns, in so far as the churches themselves have fallen prey to culturally dominant 'instrumental values' (rather than helping shape social values), little resistance to rationalizing technology is likely to appear from that quarter.

True, the huge literature of technology critique which has piled up especially since the 1960s has not been particularly Christian in character, with the prominent exception of Jacques Ellul's jeremiads. (In Europe, the 'Frankfurt School' has been conspicuous here; in the USA one thinks above all of Lewis Mumford.) Ellul takes up some strongly Weberian themes, concentrating particularly on the ascendancy of 'technique'-oriented modes of action and thought. Mere means are translated into pseudo-ends, so that, finally, 'why?' questions are eliminated. He connects this with the 'temporal' concerns of the West, whose technical movement developed in a world which had already withdrawn from the dominant influence of Christianity (Ellul, 1964). Had Christian questions been asked, he says, they would have pinpointed the issues of justice before God, and the measuring of technique by other criteria than those of technique itself.

Bearing previous comments in mind, about the relation of religion to community, it could be argued that new electronic communications media might further corrode the social bases of conventional faith. Localism and community bonds were only partially broken up by the First Industrial Revolution. But the new media encourage communal passivity (Martin, 1978, p. 92). The social centre, in such contexts, is likely to be cosmopolitan, rootless, urbanized, and thus uncongenial to the kind of active local participation on which at least New Testament Christianity depended.

Does all this mean that technology—and particularly information technology—has an inbuilt secularizing tendency? Clearly, different levels of analysis are involved. But the most patent challenge exists at the level of consciousness. Computer scientist and computer critic Joseph Weizenbaum warns that we are moving, culturally, 'from judgement to calculation' in the way we use computers (1984). There is a tendency to assume that all problems are in principle soluble, given the correct 'input', even moral problems. This, combined with the popular fallacies about 'intelligent machines' (of which, apparently, human beings may be considered a type), amounts to a definite temporality in today's thought climate. It must be added, though, that the proportion of the population who are in danger of succumbing to such algorithmic attitudes is probably not overwhelming.

From the viewpoint of anyone worried by such warnings, the public face of the churches can only increase anxiety. For the 1970s heralded the arrival of a new religious phenomenon, the 'electronic church'. However laudable the efforts to utilize currently available media for purportedly transcendent ends, both the actual product of this 'church', and the fact that there seems to be little self-criticism or technology-critique involved, does raise the question of whether such technologies are tools or tyrants. And if the 'community' point has any substance, then the deliberate abandonment of face-to-face contact by the 'Church' is little short of suicidal. One doubts that 'computer communion' could ever be a reality, or that armchair voices could be picked up on interactive networks, such that a new (electronic) song could be sung to the Lord.

More seriously, new technologies could have a long-term impact on consciousness (as the print revolution had in its day). There is manifestly much scope for the further fragmenting and disordering of knowledge (which of course sits uneasily with Christian convictions about the unity of truth). Joseph Weizenbaum complains he is constantly confronted by students who have rejected all ways but the scientific of coming to the truth, and who just want further indoctrination. The privatizing and commercializing of information sources raises further questions as to what counts as 'information'. And the proliferation of those sources tends to reduce the plausibility of any one of them as a locus of 'truth'. In all these ways, then, the secularization of consciousness could be accelerated by the diffusion of information technology.

Weber's theory seems in some ways to be vindicated. But at this point it is worth noting two things. One, he overestimated the extent to which instrumental rationality could become dominant. As Wilson points out, the excesses of technocracy can generate disillusion and even counter-technological measures. This may involve appeal to more ancient wisdom than that usually associated with integrated circuits and cable networks. Which brings in the other point: Weber reckoned without the revival of prophecy. Microelectronics is fast becoming a favourite topic among today's iconoclasts, who denounce misplaced trust in technology.

Michael Shallis' *The Silicon Idol* (1984) is a case in point. Significantly, as is the case with several other critical assessments of information technology, this one comes from within the computer science establishment. He is no mere cranky outsider deploring the miseries of modernity. Shallis views the information revolution as a triumph of 'secular technology', in which anthropomorphized machines have been erected, and are addressed, as new deities. In other words, as well as probing the ways that new technology may contribute to the draining of 'a religious view of life' from the modern world, he also perceives the outlines of alternative faiths in the microelectronic preoccupations of the present.

New Religious Movements in Technological Society
Whatever conclusion is reached about the 'sacredness' of science or technology, there can be little doubt that the numerous novel movements thrown up by the modern world are recognizably religious. Conveniently (but somewhat clumsily) lumped together as 'new religious movements', these phenomena have apparently attracted almost as much sociological attention as sincere devotees. The reason is plain. Against all the predictions of classical theory, which foretold the demise of religion, supposedly secular societies contain significant manifestations of resilient religious growth. Societies which appear secular at the public level of social organization may be decidedly 'unsecular' at other levels.

Even leaving on one side the revival of militant Islam in modernizing Iran, or the explosive expansion of Christianity in some African and Latin American countries, one is still left with evidence of considerable religious activity in the 'advanced' societies, including the USSR. Whether the Moonies or Mormons in the USA, the (Christian) Charismatic Movement in Britain, or the growth of Baptist and Orthodox churches in the Soviet Union, all these come under the sociologists' 'New Religious Movement' (NRM) umbrella. Together they constitute a challenge both to the bleaker forecasts of a secular winter, and to the creative imagination of contemporary social analysts.

Bryan Wilson, however, takes an alternative tack. Because (as we noted at the end of chapter 3) he really only counts as 'religious' that which has a manifest social-shaping impact, NRMs are seen by him as ephemeral, transient phenomena, unlikely to provide any long-term 'value consensus'. They appear to him to have no means of socializing the second generation, and thus have necessarily limited life. Apart from the Soka Gakkai movement in Japan, which he admits provides a significant 'intermediary group' or buffer between individual and society, most NRMs perform no socially-useful function. In his more recent writings, however, Wilson does allow that important questions are raised by their existence. They do give some sense of loyalty, identity and an opportunity for commitment in a 'demoralized society' (Wilson, 1982a).

An opposite view is taken by Andrew Greeley, who sees the NRMs as evidence of the longevity of 'unsecular man' (1972). He agrees that NRMs probably have little impact on corporate structures such as the military, government, business, labour unions or the educational system. But Greeley insists that their existence represents a greater explicitness and individuality in religion, and a greater scope for free choice. This proliferation of interest in what he calls 'ultimate questions' and the sacred adds up to some solid evidence for the persistence of religion. So who is right? What is the real significance of NRMs? Can they be located within the secularization scenario, or are they an aspect of 'unsecular society'?

More than once we have seen how the processes of secularization generate problems of boundary definition. What are the limits to belief and behaviour? Is it truly the case, as Dostoyevsky said, that 'If God is dead, all is permitted'? Sooner or later, it seems, a social demand arises for the clarification of boundaries, following the dissolution or blurring of older (religiously based) landmarks. Does failure confidently to assert belief in a literal hell constitute damnable (!) heresy (see Rowell, 1974)? Does the remarriage of divorcees amount to adultery? Or even, should the old structures of the established churches continue to be supported, despite their internal subversion by bureaucracy and petty ecclesiastical politics? Are these empty shells really anything more than the fossils of a once lively religion?

All these questions — of doctrine, morals and church practice — relate in some way to the social context which has spawned the NRMs. Some NRMs, whose distant origins are in the East, such as those linked with Meher Baba or Guru Maharaj-ji, minimize doctrine or tight morality, concentrating rather on the *experience* of 'karma'. Others, such as the Charismatic Movement, which has grown up within the Christian churches, find the old boundaries of liturgy and hierarchy oppressive, and also seek a new and direct experience of God.

With regard to the American experience, Dick Anthony and Thomas Robbins believe that the current spiritual flux results from the disintegration of 'traditional dualistic moral absolutism' (1982, p. 243). That is to say, Americans have tended in the past to accept a morality allegedly rooted in the Bible, which focuses on the negative, proscribed behaviour, rather than on what is right or required. So the prohibition: 'Thou shalt not steal' was not seen to cover exploitation, profiteering and so on, thus leaving an open area of 'residual permissiveness'. In these circumstances, all sorts of things become questionable. Moreover, the American infatuation with the categories of social science has compounded difficulties: it is no longer clear that people *can* be responsible for their actions any more.

Anthony and Robbins say that two conflicting responses to this flux are seen in the NRMs. On the one hand is the moral relativism implied by some modern mysticisms. Any moral absolutism, the definite boundary, is illusory to those seeking 'karma', the state of inner peace. As one Baba devotee put it: 'I don't believe that any act is good or bad in itself. It's what's behind the act, the consciousness behind the act . . . a conscious being does nothing "right" or "wrong", a conscious being just does' (Anthony and Robbins, 1982, p. 250). The quest for such 'self-actualization' is common among the NRMs, wherever they are found. Canadian adherents to similar groups also wish to step beyond time and space into what Victor Turner calls 'liminal' (threshold, limbo) experience (Bird, 1976).

The other response is a reaction against relativism, and a renewed quest for clear-cut moral absolutes and ethical dualism. The 'Jesus People' of the 1970s, the Charismatics, the Moonies, and of course the fast-growing conservative 'New Right' churches all exhibit such tendencies. Black-and-white morality is expressed in the condemnation of TV violence, video nasties, homosexuality, pornography, and so on. Along with this is a resurgence of the belief that 'free-will' choices can make a huge difference to the outcome of events.

There seems to be an increased polarizing of these two responses in the USA, which is echoed weakly in Britain and some other European countries. Anthony and Robbins perceive a general 'normative flux' in rising crime statistics, declining voter participation, family disorganization, political delegitimation, student and taxpayer dissidence, as well as in the 'spiritual ferment'. The polarizing of responses is seen in efforts to revive the 'godly state' (following the demise of civil religion) on the one hand, and on the other in narcissistic self-absorption and unconcern with civic life.

Some may feel that this understanding of NRMs, based as it is on relatively local data, and rather short-term trends, simply begs the question. Why is 'normative flux' a feature of the post-1960s West? Not surprisingly, European observers tend to see NRMs somewhat differently. Inevitably, a few write them off as merely the products of Californian affluence and eccentricity. Others, such as Roy Wallis in his recent *The Elementary Forms of the New Religious Life* (1983), prefer to retain the old Weberian categories for a more sober and long-term slant on the NRMs.

For Wallis, the process of rationalization is the backdrop to the new religious drama. Personal identity has lost its supporting institutions in the secularization process, and 'community' has been damaged, if not lost altogether. The NRMs are thus seen as filling a social void. Wallis takes other Weberian categories in order to classify the NRMs into those which reject the 'world' (Children of God, Hare Krishna, Moonies), and those which affirm the 'world' (Scientology, Primal Therapy, Encounter Groups and so on). Wallis argues that it is superficial to see the success of NRMs only in terms of their supposed capacity to brainwash or hypnotize (on this point, see also Barker, 1984). Rather, the impersonality and loneliness bred by industrial capitalist society forms the soil for world-rejecting movements, who find their 'salvation' in community. And the same 'rational' capitalist society gives rise to movements which help people cope with it: the world-affirming NRMs. If he is right, this polarized response is yet another deeply paradoxical product of capitalist industrialism.

Illuminating though it is, the Wallis thesis still does not answer all the questions. The most obvious objection is that, whereas the older mainline churches have experienced considerable decline in membership, adherence to NRMs affects only a small minority. The functional style of argument, that the NRMs 'fill a social void' scarcely stands scrutiny. The putative 'need' for community, identity or whatever does not count as an *explanation* of the rise of NRMs. And the decline of the churches can only be a necessary, not a sufficient reason for the emergence of novel cults and coteries. (The decline of church influence is taken to be a removal of obstacles to NRM involvement, a re-drawing of the boundaries.)

In an interesting critical commentary on Wallis, Colin Campbell calls attention to the cultic context, rather than merely to the actual internal beliefs of NRMs (Campbell, 1982). Campbell introduced the term 'seekership' into sociological vocabulary. A large proportion of modern populations apparently believe religious questions to be important, but do not think that dogmatic answers to them are required. Rather, open-mindedness, individuality, and the private and polymorphous nature of belief are felt to be more important than the actual content of belief. In a sense, as Campbell observes, this is roughly what Ernst Troeltsch once predicted, that 'spiritual—mystical' religion would become increasingly important in the modern world. It also resonates with the suggestions made by 'post-industrial' (or now 'information society') theorists that the reduced time spent on 'necessary labour' in the advanced societies makes space for increased 'expressive' concerns. So it is because a growing number of people are in a state of 'seekership' that the NRMs appeal. By the same token, of course, it would follow that people in these circumstances would be more prepared to believe anything, including the pronouncements of secular and political organizations.

Campbell also calls us back to Weber's different conceptions of 'rationalization'. While it can mean that efficiency and calculation supplant older religious virtues, it may also refer to cultural symbols being drawn together under a higher principle. The emergence of the NRMs, he says, shows that it is mistaken to assume that a secular culture, independent of religion, would automatically be hostile to religion, or that freeing areas from an erstwhile religious dominance would lead inexorably to their submission to instrumentally rational criteria. It is evident, for instance, in the film industry, where rationalization has produced more fantasy, horror and science fiction, or in higher education, where elements such as Freudianism, which do not enthrone rationality, still find a place. Rationalization does not necessarily spell secularization. It may strengthen mysticism and superstition, if those are right who see expressiveness as a significant feature of 'information society'. Traditional churches may continue to lose out. But that is different from the disappearance of religion.

A Note on Eastern Europe

The most spectacular NRMs have surfaced in capitalist societies, including Japan. But other advanced societies, notably the USSR, have also witnessed a religious upsurge since the 1960s. The two main areas of growth have been among the Baptists and the Orthodox. Christel Lane has argued that while earlier growth among the Baptists is in part a response to the widespread uprooting of rural communities in the course of rapid industrialization, the more recent expansion relates to the perceived failure and moral decadence of Marxist-Leninism (1982). Likewise the new involvement by young intellectuals in Orthodoxy seems to be connected with the apparent spiritual bankruptcy of the state ideology, along with a desire to discover older cultural roots.

Lane points out that there are some important differences between the 'NRMs' of Eastern Europe and those of the West, despite their roughly parallel growth since the 1960s. Firstly, Russians often regard themselves as belonging by birth to a traditionally Christian (Orthodox) culture, and religious pluralism, though present, is undeveloped. Religion is taken seriously, not as a mere consumer good, and relates more to a spiritual or mystical life rather than to ethical guidance in the present world. Secondly, individualism is not such a dominant cultural trait in the USSR as it is in the USA or UK, so the West's plethora of self-actualizing new religions has little appeal. Thirdly, it is impossible to set up the institutional frameworks which buttress Western-style NRMs within the militantly atheistic context of the USSR. Registered churches, who do not actively proselytize, find survival hard enough. The 'free market for religion' such as is found in the USA, is simply unknown.

Although the 'NRMs' of the Soviet Union are not therefore comparable with the NRMs of capitalist societies, they do once again provide evidence that the 'rationalized' society is not necessarily non-religious. The USSR is highly rationalized in some respects (Lenin was an early and enthusiastic proponent of Taylorism — the 'scientific management' of factories and farms), but neither this fact, nor extensive anti-religious propaganda campaigns (Powell, 1975) has significantly dampened religious enthusiasm, old or new.

Rationalization, Ritual and Common Religion
It cannot be repeated often enough: one's understanding of secularization depends on how religion is defined. In this chapter we have looked at the ways in which rationalization has failed to create a monolithically secular society. But some further evidence which might be presented for the 'unsecular society' theorem will be unacceptable to those who prefer to work with a narrow definition of religion. While one can live with that (I think that there is sufficient evidence even on a narrow definition), at certain points fuzziness seems unavoidable. The final section of this chapter draws attention to this fuzzy zone, by focusing on ritual and 'common religion'. It also provides a lead-in to the following chapter, which explores the implications for secularization studies of an altogether broader definition of religion.

Few would disagree that orange-robed figures swaying through the streets and chanting 'Hare Krishna' are engaging in religious ritual. These people are using their bodily movements in a symbolic fashion to articulate meaning. Likewise the action of parents bringing a child to the font for christening would be seen as a religious ritual. But what is the intrinsic difference between the 'Hare Krishna' chanters and the 'ritual' slogans and chants of an ebullient football crowd? And what if the christening meant less to our couple as an 'entry' into the established Church than as a socially accepted tradition, failure to comply with which might invite social opprobrium?

Ritual transcends the boundaries of conventional religion, and even ritual which at first glance is patently religious may have social aspects which are in fact more important for the participants. By Weberian criteria ritual action should be one of the casualties of the rationalized society. But ritual shows few signs of dying so easily. In fact, the uncoupling (differentiation) process, which in some areas has stranded 'religion' in the private sphere, seems rather to have distributed ritual across the whole spectrum of social life. So, for example, 'life-cycle' rituals, which in earlier times might have been exclusively associated with conventional religion, may now be found both inside and outside the Church. In neither case, however, has their expressive symbolism been corroded by the acid of formal rationality.

Until recently, ritual attracted scant sociological attention, mainly because it was assumed to be a victim of rationalization. One of the first to rectify this was Robert Bocock (1974). Partly influenced by Freud's insistence on the significance of the 'unconscious' life, Bocock demonstrates the inherent reductionism of sociologies which fail to take seriously that aspect of *la vie sérieuse*. He makes an analytic distinction between four overlapping types of ritual: religious, civic, life-cycle and aesthetic. But he warns against an over-cognitive approach to something which has a vital emotional dimension. Ritual is often a way of coping with life-crises, and of expressing feelings. Almost by definition, then, ritual eludes the mesh of calculative rationality.

By marshalling the evidence for the persistence of ritual in industrial society, Bocock hangs yet another question mark over the all-pervasiveness of rationalization. He looks at civic ritual, the symbolism which is vital to the maintenance of national or local identity, and points up the social significance of rituals like flag-waving and defence posturing. He devotes considerable space to showing how the rituals of the counter-culture developed in part as reactions to the one-dimensionality of life, and sometimes also as challenges to the 'dead' ritual of the traditional churches. And he examines the rituals associated with the life-cycle—birth, puberty, marriage and death. All these latter items are key points at which social structure connects with the biological growth and decay of bodies. It would be truly surprising if Western society had at last discovered ways of transcending the mysteries and crises associated for instance with death! Bocock's forceful argument is that we have not. Ritual lives on in the rational society.

What, then, of 'common religion'? Readers will recall that this is the category which straddles conventional religion and superstition. It is the 'faith' of the common people, revealed in the practices and rituals of everyday life. Such 'folk' religion has persisted in Europe for centuries, and evidence of versions of it is available in the USA. Holy wells and beliefs about black cats or walking under ladders are mixed in what appears to those used to conventional religion to be a haphazard fashion with items from recognizable Christian creeds. Some of Bocock's rituals are of course associated with such 'common' or 'folk' religion.

Witchcraft and magic provide fine examples of common religion. Each has existed alongside official religion, and borrows bits for its own purposes. Superstition clearly is still a vibrant feature of modern life; witness the evidence of popular obsession with zodiac signs and horoscopes. A tell-tale clue recorded by one social surveyor came from a respondent who 'appeared to have no metaphysical belief': ' "Have you ever consulted an astrologer?"—"No". "A palmist?"—"No". "A fortune-teller?"—"No". "Anyone else like that?"—"Only a doctor" ' (quoted in Towler, 1974, p. 152)!

Something worthy of study is 'out there'. The problem is, however important such religion for those who 'subscribe', it is extremely difficult to pin down. By definition, official religion and formal theology exclude it, so the categories are somewhat idiosyncratic and elusive. Furthermore, common religion is manifest in behaviour and occasionally-expressed belief—not in institutional churches. But as Robert Towler, who *has tried* to analyse common religion points out, many adherents of the churches in fact live according to their unauthorized version of Christianity. One imagines this would be so especially in circumstances where the official version has become remote from everyday life. Study of common religion might uncover layers of commitment hitherto obscured from the gaze of those with eyes only for church-oriented religion.

Here then is further evidence for 'unsecular society'. Ritual action has not fallen prey to the constricting grip of calculative rationality. The subterranean theologies of folk religion live on without the aid of professional theologians.

But even if this kind of evidence is not accepted as such, the Weberian view is still in deep difficulty. The main carriers of calculative rationality: science, technology and bureaucracy, have thus far failed to stifle other forms of rationality such as those rooted in tradition, affection or substantive values. To some extent, the opposite has occurred. The iron cage has challenged its captives to escape. The counter-culture, technology critics, new religious currents and 'believing' scientists all represent facets of social resistance to rationalization. Which means that secularization, understood in Weberian terms, has definite limits, according to the specific cultural context.

It also means that, once again, church strategy requires reappraisal. Caught in the cross-currents of rationalism (many Christians are involved in science-and-technology-related occupations) and irrationalism (an emotion-and-experience-centred 'faith' which has swept through different layers of church life since the 1960s), the Church is weakened. It is not in a strong position either to give guidance about the Christian moorings from which science and technology have drifted, or to understand and cope with the verdant varieties of non- and anti-rational cultures which flourish today. The social self-understanding which the exploration of 'secularization' fosters suggests that both such strategies should be strengthened if the Church is to salt the earth effectively in the late twentieth century.

But it seems somewhat unsatisfactory to leave things there, with a negative critique of both secularization sociology and the Church. Perhaps Weber and his followers are badly wrong in some respects. Perhaps the notion of 'unsecular society' should be more widely entertained. But it does beg further questions. In Weberian light, religion still appears as an epiphenomenon, or at least as only a dispensable feature of human society. Perhaps the corollary of 'unsecular society' is that religion is really central to the constitution of society. Perhaps 'sacralization studies' ought also to feature on the agenda. The consequences for 'secularization' of this alternative theorem are explored in the next chapter.

6: Social Citadels of Hope

> Israel has forgotten his Maker
> and built palaces;
> Judah has fortified many towns (Hosea 8.14).

The problem with 'secularization' is not that it is a false notion, but that it has all too often been discussed without reference to its partner, 'sacralization'. People, things, events and processes are bestowed with 'sacred' status, even as the tide of Christian influence ebbs from Western societies. The critical biblical word for this is 'idolatry', although other less offensive terms are used in sociology!

This chapter explores some of today's sacred themes, from the nation-state to sexuality, noting that they have in common a commitment to human autonomy or self-direction. In particular, we look at ways in which the decade of the 1960s was so crucial for cultural—religious change. The sacred boundaries shifted decisively during this time, with consequences for the rest of the twentieth century. And we also adjust the focus once more to get a close-up view of one such important shift; that involving women and feminism.

You hear it all the time. 'He's fanatical about football'. 'She worships her grandchildren'. 'I adore that rural landscape'. 'They gather around the flickering screen which sits like the family shrine in the living room'. 'He puts all his faith in the Dow-Jones/FT share index'. 'Western societies seem to put great store by their new "silicon idol" '. 'Scientism is knowledge which believes in itself'.

Is this mere picture-language and memorable metaphor? Or does it count as religious reality? Reinhold Niebuhr once said that, faced with the evil, suffering and enigmas of life, humans have a choice of responses. Most people opt, not for despair, but for a 'citadel of hope built on the edge of despair' (quoted in Yinger, 1970, p. 8). We must now explore some contemporary 'social citadels of hope', the 'sacred themes' of modern society. The forms these take vary from the nation-state to the wilderness to sexuality, but one thing they have in common is an association with human autonomy or self-direction. It is in this sense that they are *social* citadels: they are socially-constructed.

How does this social process of making things sacred — 'sacralization' if you like — connect with the main theme of secularization? While the ghost of vulgar secularization theories (the 'strong story' as I call it elsewhere) has been convincingly laid by Martin, Greeley, Fenn, Cox and others, some of its underlying assumptions do live on, and return to haunt us. Prominent among these is the idea that the relative decline of church influence — the receding steeple's shadow — and the rise of rational organization of life — the iron cage — means that somehow religion is a rarer phenomenon today.

Certainly, in many Western societies church-oriented religion has either partially contracted or lost its public-sphere punch (notable exceptions notwithstanding). Equally certainly, secular — that is, temporal, human-centred — outlooks and practices dominate the realms of big business, government, industry, military, communications and education. Here, the reliability of knowledge is guaranteed by science, responsibility to employees governed by cost-effectiveness and risks to the innocent and the vulnerable justified in the name of security or freedom-of-choice. Secularity also spills over into private spheres; think of women's 'control of their own bodies', family planning, men's applying 'management' ideas in home-life, and so on. In these and other senses, 'secularization' is an appropriate and apparently indispensable word.

The danger is that 'secularization' makes us unprepared for new manifestations of 'religious' life. Yet, as Martin Marty puts it, faith is more likely to be 'relocated' than 'lost' in the process of secularization. My argument is that people, things, events, institutions and processes are bestowed with sacred status, even as the tide of Christian influence ebbs from Western societies. Moreover, we may expect such 'sacred' themes in what appear to be highly 'secular' contexts. At the end of the chapter we look at feminism in this light. I question the popular Christian assumption that feminism is simply a 'secular' movement. It both has some roots in important Christian themes and church history, and simultaneously, in its 'secular' form, betrays itself as a new focus of sacred concern.

The reason for this 'sacred secularity' lies in the affinity between what in sociology we call 'sacred themes', and what in biblical language is described (and denounced!) as 'idolatry'. Human self-direction and unaided autonomy involves, biblically, a rejection of divine direction. Idolatry—or the emergence of new sacred themes—follows quickly, as in the story of kingship in Israel (the ruler is divine) or of Babel (where technology was sacred). The underlying philosophical premise is that humans beings are rightly thought of as *homo religiosus*. The designation *homo sapiens* leaves open the possibility that we are little more than intelligent machines or animals who walk upright on two legs. But as *homo religiosus,* humans are chronically involved in a quest for meaning, as seen in our creating sets of symbols, and designating certain life-areas 'sacred'. The more rationalist accounts of secularization betray their reliance on the former view. In what follows, *homo religiosus* is taken more seriously.

Let me stress that this is no simplistic 'functionalism' in which new religions arise to 'fill the vacuum' created by the diminution of conventional religious institutions. (For one thing, new, non-Christian 'sacreds' can flower *within* the Church.) Nor are we abandoning the tighter definition of religion used in discussions of secularization, which some take to be the corollary of this view (Robertson, 1978, pp. 267 – 9). Rather, we try to discover ways in which people actually seek meaning, hope and salvation in the modern world. This involves using tools which are today being developed under the term 'cultural analysis', and to which we turn attention first of all. Using these tools, secondly, we focus on the profound cultural—religious shifts of the 1960s as a background to understanding the present. For it was during that brief decade that the sacred boundaries shifted decisively, with consequences for the rest of the century.

Religion Beyond the Churches?
For Clifford Geertz, religion is a form of cultural system. It is the means by which we cope with our human limits. Religion is most clearly found at the boundaries of our ability to explain things, to cope with suffering, or to make moral choices or ethical decisions. Neither common sense, nor science, nor aesthetics can themselves yield what religion

offers. But religion is not just a 'response'. It is, in today's jargon, 'proactive', not merely reactive. That is, it actually motivates human action. Religion, as Thomas Luckmann sees it, both refers to everyday life and also points to a realm which transcends that everyday life. It helps to hold together and make sense of the routines of everyday life, and also to put its crises into a wider context. This is 'natural religion' (see chapter 1).

The symbolic universe, whether or not we wish to designate it 'religious', connects humans to the 'beyond', to the world of transcendence and mystery. It may do so in a number of ways, for example by taming it, as science tries to do in the Western tradition, or by embracing it, in the quest of ecstatic experience. But it also orients life here-and-now by providing boundaries or, better, 'landmarks' (Bernice Martin, 1981, p. 6). By it, we know what is right and wrong, true and false, acceptable and proscribed.

Of course, symbolic universes are subject to alteration, and this in a sense is exactly what this book is all about. The advanced societies, with their relative affluence, freedom and individuality have eroded traditional social rootedness and the structures of belonging once considered 'natural'. The boundaries have been removed. Less emphasis on necessity — the need to make ends meet, to survive — has meant more stress on experience, on expressiveness. But as it only seems possible to be a whole, expressive person within the privatized family, this produces conflicts. The place of learning limits, relationships, roles, is also expected to be the crucible for trying out new styles of spontaneity and restructuring. Hence the 'cultural contradictions of capitalism' (Bell, 1976). Capitalist industrialism requires the calculated organization of life for efficiency in the public realm, whereas self-fulfilment and 'doing one's own thing' is the rule of the private sphere.

Without doubt, Christianity may be viewed as a 'symbolic universe'. Western societies have to a greater or lesser degree developed with reference to its symbols and institutional forms. Today, many continue to make sense of everyday life and to put its crises into a wider context which derives from Christian (and other formal religious) commitment. But the fact that such commitment has become somewhat marginal to the organization of modern societies, or that they have themselves been infected by secularity, does not mean we simply discover 'islands of religion in a sea of secularism' (Luckmann, 1967, p. 23). On the contrary, says Luckmann, careful inquiry reveals more decisive change. New social forms of religion are taking shape to legitimate everyday life, quite beyond the lich-gate and chapel door. Luckmann's tentative forecast of the demise of 'institutionally specialized religion' is not, on present showing, likely. But his observation that, in modern societies, meaning tends to be related only to the split segments of life, rather than to life as a whole, is significant.

Both industrialism *and* capitalism have contributed to this. The bonds of local community become rather fragile, but capitalism also tends to turn everyday life into a mere routine, denuding it of moral meaning. Relationships with both nature and community are strained under these circumstances. By turning work into mere paid employment, any normative connection between work and the rest of life is severed. Labour is 'managed' without moral props. And by enclosing the majority of the population in artificial, manufactured space, the private realm of 'home' turns into a haven of 'reality' and meaning, a refuge from life 'out there' (Giddens, 1981, p. 150—6).

People find their identity in the private sphere of life, not in some overarching context. 'Consumer preference' and choice become more important to individuals. According to Luckmann, the 'sacred cosmos' of the advanced societies is characterized by an assortment of 'ultimate' meanings, a private rag-bag as it were of sacred themes. They are directly accessible—requiring no mediator—and are thus highly appropriate for the private sphere. Little surprise then that in these circumstances people may be said to 'worship the family' or to be 'devoted to rock music'. Familism is a particularly obvious candidate for sacred status, bestowing meaning and hope in a fragmented and precarious world.

Let me make just two criticisms of Luckmann's position. One is a charge of omission. By (rightly) concentrating on the private sacred themes, Luckmann does seem to underplay the significance of the public ideologies which have emerged in the modern world. No doubt his response would be that today's ideologies are somewhat bereft of subjective meaning for the individual. As he says, Marxist-Leninism in the USSR can hardly claim success in producing the 'new man'! One might add that the profit motive in capitalism has far less meaning for the labourer than might an injunction like 'doing things wholeheartedly for the Lord'. But investigation of the public ideology as a religious phenomenon is still worth pursuing. Such ideologies often obtain support by yoking their appeal to a 'private' sacred theme, like the family.

The other question is why Luckmann refuses to evaluate the trends which he illuminates. He recognizes that crucial issues are highlighted—a mass withdrawal to the private sphere while 'Rome burns'—but witholds comment. Yet by the very mention of such an issue he recognizes that some response is called for. And this is where 'idols' come in.

Kenneth Pike, a distinguished University of Michigan anthropologist and linguist, has drawn together the theological and the social aspects of 'symbolic universes'. He acknowledges that people grasp and organize their worlds in terms of non-linguistic as well as linguistic symbols—for instance flags, diamond rings and dollar bills. But when some temporal system of symbols becomes central to life it subtly shades into something else. If it invokes a 'kind of religious awe and submission', it is an indication of misdirection, for this attitude, Christians insist, 'should only be directed to a personal God' (Pike, 1962). If actions are based on such a temporal symbol (or system of symbols, verbal or non-verbal), and if it is the source of world-view and emotional charge, then it qualifies, biblically, as idolatry. A simiar stance is taken by Jacques Ellul in *The New Demons* (1976) and Tony Walter in *Sacred Cows* (1980).

Here, then, is the basis for a truly *critical* historical sociology of religion. Of course, the notion of idolatry, especially if applied to sensitive areas such as the family, is offensive to many. An age of pluralism and tolerance finds this hard medicine to swallow. But at this point Christian thought makes a real contribution to social analysis. If the human construction of purely temporal symbolic universes may in some cases be equivalent to idolatry, then the tenacity with which some such symbols are adhered to is more readily understandable. For idolatry is the investing of trust and hope in that which is unworthy of them, and incapable of rewarding them. Let me quickly add, however, that the Churches are not immune from such a critique themselves. Idolatry analysis may be applied incisively to the institutions

74941

which claim allegiance to the divine Iconoclast. Idolatry may be mixed with the religion of the Churches as well as constituting 'religion' beyond the Churches.

Idolatry: Public and Private

We might expect that public and private forms of religion would differ. It is a feature of the uncoupling of institutions and the fragmentation of life in the modern world. In particular, industrial capitalism fosters the split between work and leisure, work and home. But no neat taxonomy exists for hermetically separating private and public religion. Symbols often seem to operate in pairs, each one implying its opposite. 'Private' themes may weave themselves into 'public' ones, as I hinted is the case with the 'family' appearing on the political stage. Jacques Ellul argues that contemporary 'sacreds' are organized around two principal axes: technique/ sex and nation state/revolution. If he is right, then here again we see public and private themes mixed together. Having said that, the accent of each symbol still tends to be in one sphere or another, even if there is overlap.

It makes sense to begin with ideologies, which by definition are projects intended publicly to mobilize populations. They also claimed, in the nineteenth century, to have taken over from traditional religion, and there is at least *prima facie* evidence for this. Take the state. For Ellul, this has become the supreme power in the modern world. This abstract, rational entity has taken to itself the sacred status once reserved for monarchs. People look to the state as provider, as ordainer (it is, for example, supposed to ensure social security and to 'run the economy', even in post-Keynesian days). Of course, sacrifice is demanded of its citizens, especially at election time. And it may inspire awe, if not terror—think of the impact of *Nineteen eighty-four.*

But the state is only semi-sacred without its partner: nation. The nineteenth century also left a legacy of nationalism, which reached its ugliest expression in the Great War. Sacrifice—*pro patria mori*—becomes butchery in this context, even though at another level the nation state is the great organizer of the good. The state, it is claimed, acts in the 'national interest'.

Another dimension may be added to this by recalling the idea of 'civil religion'. 'God bless America' represents the most blatant expression of this, but it also has parallels elsewhere. Robert Bellah's studies of civil religion revived interest in this phenomenon (1970, pp. 168—89). He follows Rousseau in defining it as a set of vaguely defined symbols or ideals with religious connotations which help invest public life or civil government with a seemingly sacred quality. Nazi Germany patently falls into this category. South Africa, on the other hand, does not. There, one undoubtedly sees nationalism blessed by religion. The Dutch Reformed Church has been called the 'National Party at prayer'. National identity is maintained through the ruthless policy of 'separate development' or *apartheid*. State and religion are closely intertwined, and in the reference to the 'covenant' (in the celebration of 'Covenant Day', 16 December,) one finds similarities with American civil religion. But it is not the same. The most obvious reason for dissimilarity is that the sacred symbols are not shared by the majority of the population.

Nigeria may yield a better example of civil religion, although the evidence is at present fragmentary. In Nigeria religious pluralism already exists (suitable soil, in Bellah's terms, for the development of civil religion). Primal religion, Christianity, Islam and various new religious movements co-exist. Religious freedom is guaranteed by the 1979 Constitution.

Corruption and 'moral bankruptcy' (as they call it) attendant on rapid social change are felt to call for religious solutions. The main evidence that a civil religion may be forming is in the speeches of political leaders. In 1982 President Shehu Shagari called for an 'ethical revolution' because, he said, a nation without moral standards is like a body without a soul. To this end he publicly encouraged the development of 'God-given skills' to facilitate nation-building— in both Christian and Muslim contexts. This Muslim president called on all Nigerians at Christmas time to follow the humility and simplicity of Christ, as a means to making a better Nigerian society (Hackett, 1983). The Nigerian equivalent of national—religious hero Abraham Lincoln is assassinated military ruler General Murtala Muhammed. Whether or not this flowers into a civil religion remains to be seen, but the lesson is there: a non-Christendom, pluralist country may still seek a common 'religion' in the pursuit of national identity and cohesion.

Bob Goudzwaard, of the Free University of Amsterdam, has suggested how 'idolatry' and 'ideology' analysis are related (1984). Legitimate national goals become ideological, he says, when the means of reaching them are treated as if they were ends in themselves. That is to say, when the means are idolized. Thus the goal of generating sufficient economic activity to ensure an adequate standard of living for all citizens may become the ideology of progress via material prosperity and economic growth. Technology may be regarded as the means of reaching this goal. But it all-too-easily loses its status as a mere means to an end, and takes on a transcendent dimension as a cure-all, an idol which is both revered and feared. Thus ideology may be considered as the 'conduit of idolatry'.

Many commentators concur with Ellul in seeing revolution as another modern 'sacred' which makes a pair with the 'state'. This is a sacred of transgression, set over against the sovereign power of the state. Love of the state is countered by hatred of it. And this is an ongoing phenomenon. Revolution is no longer a moment. For its adherents, it is a continuing confrontational way of life. If not before, this became very clear from the time of the 1960s Trotskyite commitment to 'permanent revolution'. This modern myth (as Berger calls it, 1977) is as attractive in post-colonial situations in the Third World (where foreign states are the opposing sacred) as it is in isolated conspiratorial cells in Europe and North America. If revolt succeeds, such is the insatiable appetite of the revolutionary that it tends to become dogmatically ideological. The idol must be kept alive, even if ideals such as freedom are betrayed.

We turn now to look at what Luckmann identifies as likely foci of sacred concern. Mainly in the private realm, they also find resonance in the public sphere. For instance, sexuality is not a public sphere 'sacred' like the state, but it is nonetheless exploited in the public sphere via advertising and the media.

For Luckmann, the assortment of ultimate meanings and sacred themes which could add up to new social forms of religion all relate to individuals, and are inherently unstable. Ultimate significance is found in individual autonomy. Historically, this is rooted in Romanticism, finds its expression in the new capitalist *bourgeoisie* of the nineteenth and twentieth centuries, and is negatively mirrored in bohemianism and the 'counter-culture'. Autonomy is associated with the absence of external restraint and traditional taboo (and is thus partially consequent upon the corrosion of the codes of Christendom). Autonomy means self-set boundaries, or in some cases the proclamation that there are no boundaries.

Sacred themes, seen thus, include various movements and teachings related to self-expression and self-actualization, as manifest in everything from educational policy to tabloid advice columns. The mobility ethos, with its sense that the environment is infinitely manipulable by humans, and which spurns rootedness and public sociality, is another of Luckmann's 'sacreds'. The autonomous individual has a youthful if not eternal quality, which means that death is not really part of the new sacred themes. Personal health could also be considered as a new sacred. According to a 1983 Gallup Poll, British people now value health *above* family life. More than twice as many people are worried by health-related issues than in 1966 (thrèe times as many as in 1951) (*New Society,* 15 July 1983, p. 104). The rising incidence of cancer seems significant here; at least one courageous Canadian cancer victim has become a cultural hero via public feats of stamina and endurance such as long-distance walking.

Two other noteworthy sacred themes already alluded to are familism and sexuality. The family became a major element of political platforms on both sides of the Atlantic in the 1970s. This represents an appeal to an existing centre of concern (which of course has the effect of amplifying that concern). However, the family in question is essentially the '*bourgeois*' family, the type of nuclear family which has emerged alongside industrialism. (Which is not to say it is a *product* of industrialism! The nuclear family in fact antedates capitalist industrialism.) Herein lies another contradiction. Individualism and the autonomy quest may also infiltrate the family. A tension builds up between the family ideal and individuals who wish to function independently within it.

The fact that the family is subject to intense hostility itself lends weight to the belief that 'family' is idolized. The 1960s spawned a virulent anti-family sentiment, which blames the family for much oppression and inhibition. This is another 'sacred of transgression', deliberately trampling previously accepted boundaries. Its presence paradoxically complicates the task of commentators who wish to expose family idolatry without being tarred with the same brush as anti-familists. (As Tony Walter found when he pointed out that moralists often denounce the idols of money and sex before contrasting them with 'good' things like work and the family (1980, p. 47). His point is that work and family idolatry infects the Church.)

Sexuality is a favourite candidate for sacred status (see, for instance, Michel Foucault's isolating of sexuality as a focus of post-Christian worship, 1980). When sex is severed from procreation by contraception, and when family and kinship become less important to the maintenance of the economy (rules of inheritance and so on), it is open to deregulation in the private sphere. This is more or less what has happened in the West. It enters the stage as a crucial element in the autonomous individual's quest for self-fulfilment.

Ellul, curiously, sees sex as a sacred to be counterposed with sacred technology. He thinks moderns feel so hopelessly trapped in the 'iron cage' of technique that they desperately light upon sexuality as a means of liberation. The neat orderliness of calculation and efficiency is desacralized by sexual transgression. Sexuality is explored as a means of life-transformation. But as idolatry takes over, it appropriates the very technique it purportedly rejects, becoming subject to obsession with performance and success. Sex manuals, sex therapy, and sex counselling all bear witness to this. Freedom, it seems, would be better sought *from,* rather than *in* sexuality, seen this way. Idols never liberate.

Symbolic Sea-Change?

Having examined several possible candidates for new sacred themes, or idolatries, we turn now to a more concrete investigation of contemporary — post-1960 — society. The 1960s were a decisive decade for cultural-religious change (the 1870s were similarly critical last century). The 1960s generated the so-called counter-culture and the new religious movements. Talcott Parsons dubbed it an 'expressive revolution' (this idea is discussed with great acumen by Bernice Martin, 1981; see also Arthur Marwick, 1982, chapter 9).

This symbolic sea-change connects profoundly with secularization themes. The effects of modernity, not least secularization, were felt powerfully in the 1960s. The 'uncoupling' of social institutions seemed so to have fragmented and atomized life that people despairingly sought modes of 'reintegration'. In Britain, the Church of England could no longer be considered a 'national church', and in other countries also, the period after the Second World War formed a watershed between eras. The rationally-planned economy and society was paramount.

But if rational planning, technology and bureaucracy were the order of the day, then many symbols and rituals emerged to articulate alternatives to them. Questioning the 'obvious' benefits of science and technology became part of that 'alternative' way of life. Of course, the counter-culture, with its hippies, communes and Zen Buddhism, attracted only a minority of serious devotees. But the rituals and symbols born at that time appealed to a much broader constituency, expressing for many who remained in 'straight' or '*bourgeois*' life a form of consciousness and modes of action which were repelling poles to the dominant technological climate.

Those who dismiss the counter-culture as a juvenile reflex of Californian affluence should note the way that 'counter-cultural' themes have become acceptable today. Friends of the Earth, Greenpeace, various campaigns for nuclear disarmament and for the politics of ecology, feminism and women's liberation, food and educational co-operatives, and appropriate technology all bear witness to the permeation of public life by the kinds of values and attitudes which once were seen as the domain of the counter-culture. Who in the 1950s would have believed that 'Transcendental Meditation' would take its place within high school curricula? As Martin says, 'In the last few decades the Western world has experienced a transformation in the assumptions and habitual practices which form the cultural bedrock of the daily lives of ordinary people' (1981, p. 1).

The advanced societies' drive towards urban industrial existence took away a sense of rootedness, belonging and acceptable behaviour at the same time as the churches underwent rapid marginalization. So as social boundaries and frameworks were expanded (female nudity, for instance, went decidedly public, in shops and daily newspapers) little acceptable guidance was available to determine the new limits. As George Grant says of Canada, 'the Church was no longer the keeper of the nation's conscience, and few Canadians seemed to regret its dethronement' (in Slater, 1976). But this secularization does not necessarily mean that the new frameworks were entirely non-religious. Bernice Martin remarks that the anti-materialism and anti-instrumentality which flourished from the 1960s onwards formed the 'locus of the sacred' for the cultural class which embodied them (1981, p. 17).

Let me summarize one or two of Martin's most telling points. Firstly, she sees two factors which ensured the 'success' of the 'counter-culture' in incorporating itself into mainstream culture. One links with the idea that there is a 'new class' of 'expressive professionals' (in education, therapeutic and media occupations), created by a split within the old middle class. One means of gaining a foothold was simply that family and other connections meant that the 'new class' is still close to the cultural élite of the power centre. The other factor has to do with the process of legitimation in advanced societies, in which the sacred centre gives way to attack from the periphery by accommodating to aspects of it. So earlier disruptive tactics have given way to more routine methods of 'pressure group' activity. This suggests how the boundaries are relocated, and fits nicely with Fenn's proposal that secularization occurs as a sort of contest between different groups struggling to define the sacred/secular boundary.

The symbolism of the 'expressive revolution' is 'anti-structure', the desire to get rid of or transcend what are felt to be superfluous, constricting and maybe oppressive limits to human activity. Form and ritual were attacked in the 1960s—and new ones were made. School uniforms, the 'BBC accent', and different clothes for men and women all were questioned. Of course, it is vital to note the variations of 'counter-cultural' impact, especially between classes. In the more traditional enclaves of European and North American society, taken-for-granted styles of dress, speech and behaviour have persisted, and to this day are less affected by the 'expressive revolution'. Among such groups, outrage and offence at such cultural assault is, understandably, more common.

The most prominent vehicle for the transmission of 'liminoid' (boundary-questioning) culture is rock music and, more generally, what is usually referred to as 'youth culture'. Not thought and calculation, but play and experience are the outstanding qualities of 'rock'. Not cerebral but celebratory. The messages of rock music are overwhelmingly hedonistic — but nevertheless carry their own 'orderliness' with them. Today, frustrations and disappointment not unrelated to youth unemployment are expressed in the nihilism of 'punk', which seems to proclaim not just that boundaries should expand but that they should explode. It is not hard to see how such liminal disorder may also be an expression of the sacred.

The concern with self-expression and self-actualization remarked above is a key motif of the 'expressive revolution' and its cultural legacy. Bernice Martin joins cultural critics such as Christopher Lasch and Richard Sennett in unapologetic excoriation of such 'narcissistic' tendencies. Having the autonomous self as the sacred centre of cultural gravity extorts a heavy price in competitiveness, isolation and rootlessness. Even in communes, where human togetherness is officially prized, there is evidence that the 'possessive individualism' so characteristic of the capitalist ethos is corrosive of community (Abrams and McCulloch, 1976).

In the next chapter, some aspects of the 'symbolic sea-change' are revisited, in particular the relation of the official guardians of the sacred (the clergy) to the rise of expressive professions. But in order once more to demonstrate both the relevance and the complexity of discussing secularization in the modern context, we isolate one further aspect of contemporary cultural change, the women's movements.

Women: Looking for a New Home?

The symbolism of anti-structure, so central to the expressive revolution, is picked out in bold relief in the women's movement. The urge to liberate women is a call to defy established structure — that of both family and occupation. Whatever the varieties of feminism, and many exist, they have in common a deep-seated hostility towards conventional family-patterns, patriarchy and discrimination. But one also hears the accents of autonomy, self-realization and possessive individualism in the female voice, not least in 'control of the body' argument for abortion rights.

The despised and defied structures are not infrequently associated with traditional Christianity. The churches bear the brunt of charges of Pauline misogyny and male superordination at a doctrinal level, and a frozen career structure which excludes women from serious responsibility, at a practical level. The teaching of the Church is taken to spell support for the family, as the locus of male dominance, female unpaid (and thus unacknowledged) labour, and the transmission of stereotyped sex-roles to the next generation. Because these items figure prominently in feminist polemic, the movement appears to bristle with secularist threat. Christian integrity is at stake.

At the same time, the threat also challenges society itself. The landmark removers are at work, redefining the very boundaries which are essential to stable civilization. Those relationships which in some ways had taken on a sacredness of their own—such as the family—are desacralized *in the name of a new sacred!* So a double process is at work. On the one hand the supposedly monolithic teaching of the churches, and thus any residual social influence held by them, is attacked by feminism. On the other, the sacredness of certain institutions is denied, and female human power is asserted as a new sacred.

Visible in the American 'new right' one can discern both strands. On the one hand, opposition to the 'Equal Rights Amendment' is held up as an expression of Christian resistance to the would-be destroyers of marriage and family. On the other, secularist infiltration of the Church is suspected in the subversive activities of Christian feminism. The issue is symbolically dovetailed with that of biblical authority. Those who do not find male supremacy and domestic womanhood in the Bible have a 'low view of Scripture'. Of course, as Richard Fenn observes, the biblical question is crucial. 'Has God said . . .?' is the opening gambit of more than one unilateral declaration of independence (1982, p. x). The Church can dig its own grave by casting radical doubt upon its own documents. The point I am making is that many 'new right' type Christians, especially in the USA, assume that this is what all Christian feminists are up to.

As soon as these questions are placed within a longer

historical frame, the 'women's movement as secularizing force' idea acquires even greater nuance. One finds, for instance, that some of the supposed Christian associations with the '*bourgeois* family' are in fact unintended consequences of particular circumstances. In feudal and early capitalist times, the establishment of paternity was crucial to the transmission of property. Religion was used ideologically as a means of regulating sexual practice—especially marriage. Thus where religion appeared as a means of controlling women's bodies, anyone who dared to seek emancipation had to struggle against popular versions of religious conceptions of sexuality (Turner, 1983, pp. 236ff). In Italy, this is still very much how things are seen.

Other unintended connections between religion and sexuality include practices like the 'churching of women'. 'Churching' is a ceremony in which women who have recently experienced childbirth are reaccepted into the congregation. Christian churches have had an ambiguous stance towards this practice, originating as it probably does in pagan ritual (and thus a component of 'common religion'). Yet it is precisely this kind of practice which is singled out by today's feminists to show how the male-dominated religious system sets women apart and only reintegrates them into the community on certain terms (Rushton, 1983). The fact that women frequently collude with this by actually asking for 'churching' does nothing to mitigate the association of Church with repression.

Sexuality is hardly connected with public legitimation today. In fact, as Foucault comments, it now points to nothing beyond itself, having also been cut off from procreation and marriage through the technologies of birth control. Yet one could argue that it is vulnerable to sacralization in more than one way. As far as women are concerned, the personal control of bodies (manifest for instance in the obsession with trim torsoes, formerly via cosmetics, now through exercise) may well reach an idolatrously symbolic high.

To return to the women's movement, another historical observation is in order. A simple correlation of feminism with secularism is hard to square with nineteenth-century evidence. Despite the social conservatism which tended to constrain female activities in Church as in society, a number of English evangelicals showed the same kind of emancipatory fervour regarding women as they had with slaves in an earlier period (Banks, 1981). They attacked male dominance, peppering their manifestoes with biblical precedent (see Bebbington, 1984). Early Methodists and the Salvation Army gave leadership roles to women which the female faithful (except among Quakers) had not known for centuries. Likewise in the USA, the women's movement made significant strides under evangelical leadership (Dayton, 1976, pp. 85—6). Charles Finney, the revivalist, contributed to this by insisting on the biblical privilege of women's praying and testifying in public (Harrison, 1975). Without judging the wisdom of some of these moves, we clearly find here well-intentioned Christian groups and churches in the vanguard of emancipation. At the very least, they hung question marks over the complacent assumption of male superiority. Of course, these feminisms were pro-family—a far cry from some contemporary counterparts (not of Christian origin) which doubt the necessity of any formal heterosexual relationship for the nurture of children.

What such historical examples also demonstrate is the folly of assuming any simple one-way relation between 'social movements' such as feminism, and the churches. What may appear to some today as the permeation of 'secular' ideas into the churches has a nineteenth-century precedent which was quite the other way round! The 'secular' movements were initiated or boosted by the 'religious'. However, it is probably accurate to say that the churches in the 1960s and 1970s were caught with their platitudes down, rather unprepared for the impact of the (often un-Christian) women's movement. Thus today confusion exists within the would-be Christian feminist camp. One party accepts a secular agenda, and in blessing it assumes that churches should have 'career structures' like any comparable non-religious organization. Bureaucratic synods listen to this view, as it accords with their *modus vivendi.* The other works from a biblical base, prophetically attacking misinterpretations of Scripture and the unthinking allegiance to cultural codes as if they were authentically Christian.

Are feminists 'looking for a new home'? This idea is deliberately ambiguous. Feminists clearly reject much of what has passed as 'home' life. And yet by subjecting their activities to a 'cultural analysis' approach, we may see that in redrawing the boundaries, feminism is in a sense searching for a new (metaphysical) home. A new ideology, a new identity: aspects of feminism may be interpreted as pointing to a new 'citadel of hope', a contemporary sacred theme. Social movements often build around themselves a symbolic universe— frequently with overtones of human autonomy—which have a distinct aura of religiosity about them.

Even if this interpretation is unacceptable, the case of feminism certainly shows how complex is the secularization debate. It gives weight to the 'social action' approach to secularization studies, in that one may clearly see here a contest between parties and groups each wishing to define the sacred/secular boundary for themselves. This issue of where the boundaries lie is of central importance if we are to understand the complex issues of religion, culture and society. This is so whether or not one accepts that some symbols are equivalent to 'idols'. However, if there is a sense in which new sacred themes have an affinity with what from a Christian viewpoint are objects of *false* devotion, then this raises additional challenges for the churches quite beyond those already thrown up by secularization.

7: Secularization: a Crisis for Christianity?

> From the religious point of view, humanity has entered a long night that will become darker and darker with the passing of the generations and of which no end can yet be seen. It is a night in which there seems to be no place for a conception of God, or for a sense of the sacred, and ancient ways of giving significance to our own existence, of confronting life and death, are becoming increasingly untenable (Acquaviva, 1979, p. 202).

Secularization is both a challenge and a threat to the survival of authentic Christianity. It means that Christianity appears to be a minority opinion (among many others) held by individual members of a socially marginal institution whose widespread influence in the West is a thing of the past. Its claim to be true and ever-relevant is doubted both because society operates without the assistance of the Church and because the Church is all too often indistinguishable from the rest of society.

Italian Catholic Sabino Acquaviva is not the only one to foresee a long night, getting progressively darker. American Moral Majority leader Jerry Falwell also has a gloomy outlook for society if modern secularity persists much longer. In fact, anyone sympathetic to Christian faith, who seriously takes stock of the secular situation, is bound to have some fears for the future. Not only are pressures perceived from outside the churches (such as a loss of power or prestige; the result of being 'uncoupled' from the state), but also, internally, the churches are still 'by schisms rent asunder'. For instance, rifts develop as certain groups are suspected of reducing the gospel to a purely temporal dimension by making its political dimension its *raison d'être*.

In this chapter we turn the spotlight on the churches to assess what a re-examination of secularization means for them. We firstly survey the standard evidence for religious

114

vitality, involvement in conventional religious practice. Growing numbers of people staying away from church is one indicator of secularization. But so is the invasion of a rational calculating mentality into church life, and that is far harder to gauge. Secondly, we look at the best-known formulation of the difficulties faced by churches in a contemporary context, Peter Berger's ideas on accommodation or resistance to secularization. Thirdly, the position of the clergy is singled out for attention; it neatly illustrates some of these wider questions.

So, in what senses may secularization be considered a crisis for Christianity? The stance taken here is that secularization should both be taken seriously, and be seriously criticized. So without sidestepping the gauntlets thrown down by secularization, we also suggest how this idea may obscure the options and opportunities paradoxically offered to the Church in the modern world.

Pews, Prayer and Participation
Gallup polls are not the best instrument for discerning life in the Spirit. Nevertheless such polls do fascinate many social analysts and historians. Hot dispute arises, for instance, over how trade fluctuations affect church life. Holders of the 'soup kitchen' theory believe people attach themselves to churches in hard times in order to benefit from philanthropy, while their opponents object that in fact 'cost consciousness' becomes more significant during a depression, and people prefer to place their money elsewhere than in the offering box. Many similar supposed correlations simply cancel each other out.

Yet this 'figures fascination' infects para-church organizations as well. Many a church growth consultant is hooked on statistical tables as indices of the salvation of souls. As far back as 1851, Horace Mann's report of a mere 7.3 million adults in church out of a possible 13.5 million called forth shocked heart-searching. Today's (probably generous) estimate that less than 25 per cent attend church regularly in England would no doubt have caused him heart *failure.* (Only 13 per cent of eligible people in England even *claim* to be church members (Brierley, 1982).) Now, as then, the statisticians' instruments are crude, and the results, even if not downright misleading, often produce strange paradoxes.

What, for instance, are we to make of the findings of pollsters in the 1940s and 1950s in the USA that for many religion meant less in life, and yet at the same time church attendance was increasing?

In a very general way, of course, social statistics do yield an overall picture at least of institutional vitality in a given setting. While frankly recognizing the folly of appealing to percentages when assessing the power of faith, some sociologists make a good case for a limited reliance on statistical inquiry (see Martin, 1978, p. 13). From such figures one learns that, whatever the *meaning* of church involvement in each situation, Christianity is growing at a tremendous rate in several African countries and round the 'Pacific rim' (Singapore, Korea and so on). We also discover that Christianity not only survives, but in some cases flourishes despite official tactics designed to dismantle it in China, the Soviet Union and in other Eastern European countries. At the same time, one finds a levelling off or slippage in church adherence in several Western European and Scandinavian settings.

Needless to say, within each of these countries, the situation differs with class, cultural, generational and other factors. It also differs by region. In Britain, for instance, the Celtic fringes — Wales, Scotland, Ulster — have a higher rate of religious activity then the more cosmopolitan 'centre', and the difference is especially marked the closer one is to London and the south east. In the USA, Dean Hoge and D. A. Roozen come to the unremarkable conclusion that 'The wellsprings of Christian commitment do not seem to exist in or near the secular humanistic ethos, where intense individualism, relativism and transient commitments seem to channel spiritual energies in different directions' (1979). Another important factor is the kind of church in question. Clearly the meaning and style of church involvement varies a lot for instance between Catholics and Charismatics.

(In fact, one good reason for not including Roman Catholicism in the discussion is that in some ways it is a special case. The fairly uncompromising line possible within a church traditionally strongest in areas away from the metropolitan centres of Europe and North America is more difficult to maintain when (especially in the USA) there is Catholic strength in just those centres. The same secular threats come to Catholicism as to Protestantism, but perhaps with a time-lag (see McSweeny, 1980). In Britain and North America, both the Charismatic Movement and shifts within the Vatican have been instrumental in breaking down some barriers between Roman Catholics and Protestants, even though at a fundamental doctrinal level the rift remains. Although some British evangelicals have been embarrassed by the pollsters' demonstration of affinities between their outlook and that of Catholics, the differences still mean that Catholicism deserves separate study.)

That said, it is worth dwelling for a while on a phenomenon which has achieved increasing prominence in the past decades, namely the persistence and growth of 'conservative' Christianity in Britain and the USA. Of course, it is no novelty that evangelicals should experience revival independently of any wider resurgence of religious interest; this has happened before on both sides of the Atlantic and elsewhere. Nevertheless it is significant that the present strength is manifest at a time when all the predictions were of a general decline of religion in advanced societies.

In the 1960s the needles marking religious practice on several scales began to quiver. Roman Catholicism, which had been holding its own especially where Protestant majorities held sway, began to slip. Ecumenism, heralded after the war as the boldest organizational bulwark against the internal collapse of the Church, started to look somewhat jaded. On both sides of the Atlantic such congregations appeared to need geriatric treatment. Just at this time, when the mainline denominations began to droop, evangelicalism began to flourish.

Without the razzle-dazzle of America's 'prime-time' televangelists the stirrings of a more sedate British evangelicalism were understandably less obvious, but no less real. In Britain, it has mainly been a doctrinally-traditional, biblically-based movement, although it must be said that both the new politically active, and the Charismatic elements sometimes tug impatiently at those moorings. The professionals involved are still predominantly in medicine, business and natural science, but a strong streak of 'expressive revolution' permeation is also evidenced in the advent of 'media Christians' and Christian rock music.

In the USA, *Newsweek* hailed 1976 as 'the year of the

evangelical'. By 1982 (March 15) the rise of evangelical strength became front page headline news in the *New York Times:* 'Often overshadowed by fundamentalism and shunned by church liberals, the mainstream of evangelical Christians has emerged as the most powerful new force in American Protestantism'. At this point, an important distinction must be made between 'evangelicalism' and 'fundamentalism'. Followers of the latter tend to be biblical literalists, and are often also politically right wing. The big-time TV Christians— such as Jerry Falwell of the Moral Majority—are more often than not of this stamp. In the words of the *New York Times,* 'In essence, evangelicals stand between liberals and fundamentalists'. Of course, this is a deceptively simple distinction. Many other factors cut across it. For example, both groups have identified political concern as a valid outworking of faith. But while fundamentalists are using electronic mass mailings for what appear for all the world like Republican causes, evangelicals tend to opt for a more broadly-based quest for 'social justice'.

Whatever the precise details, the fact remains that if sociologists and historians of religion seek signs of religious life within the Christian pale (as opposed to documenting the more exotic or bizarre new religious movements), they cannot but notice the persistence, revival or resurgence of the more orthodox, biblically-based versions of Christianity. The question is, given the dominance of 'secularization' as an analytical tool, how is this trend explained? In order to answer that, however, we must first grasp the basic ideas which have influenced most such interpretations.

The Deadly Dilemma
Back in 1967, Peter Berger voiced his conviction that, faced with secularization, the churches have two main options available:

They can either accommodate themselves to the situation, play the pluralistic game of religious free enterprise, and come to terms as best they can with the plausibility problem by modifying their product in accordance with consumer demands. Or they can refuse to accommodate themselves, entrench themselves behind whatever socio-religious structures they can maintain or construct, and continue to profess the old objectivities as much as possible as if nothing had happened (Berger, 1969, p. 153).

118

This is the 'deadly dilemma'. Secularization presents Christianity with a nasty choice between being relevant but undistinctive or distinctive but irrelevant. Much may be learned by assessing actual situations with these two polar extremes in mind.

The accommodation of the Church to the world (itself a classic definition of 'secularization' (Shiner, 1967)) is, in the words of Alan Gilbert, 'the dominant trend in modern British religious history' (1980, p. 105). It is the response associated for instance with 'denominationalism'. Unlike established churches, denominations accept pluralism, and claim no exclusive authority. They are voluntary, and make no attempt to stop adherents from belonging to other organizations, or to deviate from other social norms. They may regard themselves as a sort of social conscience, but not in opposition to mainstream culture. Denominations are likely to have a bureaucratic organization, which in itself may be seen as a form of accommodation. Once travelling down that road, a business-style merger—ecumenism—becomes all the more appropriate and less open to question.

Accommodation also affects belief and ethical practice. The 'liberal' Christian stance is to accommodate to modern currents of thought and moral opinion. Bishop John Robinson's efforts in *Honest to God* to show that God really does operate 'down here' led many to conclude that for him, God is not 'out there' at all. Steve Bruce has documented ways in which the liberal 'Student Christian Movement' committed 'organizational suicide' by organizing 'bridge-building' conferences on 'Christ and Freud' or 'Christ and Marx'. Given the already equivocal beliefs about what constitutes Christian orthodoxy, the result was that 'these bridges served as paths of defection for SCM members. Rather than Marxists becoming Christians, the Christians became Marxists' (Bruce, 1984, p. 91).

The other pole is entrenchment, or resistance, one facet of which is 'sectarianism'. (In Britain such sectarianism is more likely to be outside the denominations than in the USA, where denominations can themselves be sectarian.) As Bryan Wilson shows, sects are exclusive in belief, and are essentially protest groups. They often 'come into being as intense reaffirmations of an older religious tradition' (Wilson, 1982, p. 98).

In the USA, James Hunter (1983) sees evangelicals (broadly defined) resisting 'secular humanism' above all in the area of morals and practice (although the much-publicized 'battle for the Bible' is usually lumped in with this). They are busy stemming the tide of divorce, abortion, permissiveness, women's liberation and secular schooling. This makes evangelicalism political, but the reader will recall that Hunter also subjects the phenomenon to class analysis. Evangelical members of the old bourgeoisie are steeling themselves against the unwanted incursion of the 'new class'.

This requires further investigation, in its British as well as its American form. The 'moral crusade' of the British 'Nationwide Festival of Light' whose initial flush of charisma has routinized into a political lobby (CARE Campaigns) also seems to betray an analogous class liaison. At least, the kinds of issues singled out for attention are not ones which would challenge or *offend* the *status quo* of the respectable middle classes. At the same time, it is remarkable that, after decades of quiescence in the USA and Britain, conservative Christians should be politically mobilized at all. The differences in scale between the two has to do with the way the system gags any minority voice in the UK, as opposed to the relative ease of turning such local interests into *issues* in the USA, especially with resource-backing (Bruce, 1984a, pp. 37—42).

Note that the use of the term 'middle class' is not intended to be pejorative in this context. The links between class location and religious activity are worthy of serious investigation, and do have a bearing on Christian practice. The fact that some Christian virtues (such as pre-marital chastity) happen to coincide with *some* so-called middle-class values only presents difficulties to those prejudiced against one or the other (or both). The churches have some explaining to do, however, if their outlook more nearly *mirrors* that of one discernible social stratum than another. Some current controversies between different wings of the Church could be cooled if the participants showed greater willingness to distinguish between the codes of class and the claims of Christ.

Returning to the 'deadly dilemma', then, we may see how patterns of response to perceived secularization do fit with Berger's models (or 'ideal types'). The liberal's question is 'how far can we go?', while the conservative asks, 'how strong are the defences?'. (Note again how important is the *boundary* question.) When in Britain a Baptist theological college principal denies with impunity Christ's divinity, a Methodist leader doubts the virgin birth, and an Anglican bishop questions the reality of the resurrection (although David Jenkins does say it is more than 'God's conjuring trick with bones'), this rings liberal, accommodation bells. But when ex-*Christianity Today* editor Harold Lindsell accuses self-confessed *biblical* theologians at reputable evangelical seminaries of colluding with the enemy in the 'battle for the Bible', there is the sectarian scent of 'entrenchment' in the ghetto.

The 'deadly dilemma' is visible in recent studies—to continue this theme—of conservative Christianity. James Hunter is more explicitly Bergerian in *American Evangelicalism: Conservative Religion in the Quandary of Modernity*. Steve Bruce is nevertheless aware of the 'dilemma' in his work on British 'conservative Protestantism': *Firm in the Faith*. For both of them, the scene is set by secularization, and thus the riddle to be explained is the 'survival' or 'persistence' of these forms of religion into the later twentieth century.

Hunter's 'quandary' is of course Berger's 'dilemma'. The religious world-view, faced with the juggernaut of modernity, is obliged to do some serious 'cognitive bargaining'. The resulting deal resembles either accommodation or resistance. In the first, belief is 'domesticated'. If you cannot beat the rule-bounded rationality of the dominant culture, then why not join it? Rule-bounded spirituality is the outcome of this bargaining: Campus Crusade's Bill Bright invented the 'Four spiritual laws', which reduces the gospel to a neat package, suitable for instant consumption. Numerous 'how-to' manuals line the shelves of the Christian bookstore, from marriage and family to personal fitness—'Trim for Him'.

This domestication takes other forms as well. Hunter comments on a new 'evangelical civility' which soft-pedals sin, advertises peace and joy, and seems to say 'No offence, I am an evangelical' (1983, p. 87). Subjectivism is another trait he highlights—shades of the Romantic thrust of the expressive revolution perhaps? This points up a significant change: 'The inner posture of mastery of ascetic Protestantism has given way to an inner flaccidity of a largely subjectivistically-oriented [sic!] evangelicalism' (1983, p. 99).

So faith may be made to fit modern 'needs', and is inoffensive: thus is it tamed.

The other side of the coin is resistance. Far from drawing the teeth of evangelicalism, this approach actually tries to give it teeth. Hunter pertinently draws attention to the larger context which has produced the recent focus on *moral* issues. In the first half of the twentieth century the Protestant supernaturalist understanding of the universe was under siege, but traditional morality largely remained intact within the wider population. After the Second World War, however, particularly from the 1960s onwards, that traditional morality began to dissolve. Gay liberation, divorce and abortion only became real issues then, reflecting, it is said, the breakdown of belief. A 'secularist philosophy takeover', as Senator Jesse Helms calls it, lies at the back of the collapse of moral values, especially in home and school.

The Moral Majority and Christian Voice each use the language of 'covenant', which, they say, is being dangerously flouted in America today. Their resistance to moral degeneration thus uses tradional motifs, often expressed in stark 'either/or' form. As Richard Mouw suggests, they operate with a 'Manichean' view of reality: issues are viewed in black and white only. The boundaries, the defences, are well-defined. Yet the rationale is not always so transparent. 'It is not clear', Mouw goes on, 'why the Panama Canal Treaty should figure prominently in a Christian laundry list of political concerns' (Mouw, 1981). More frightening is the assumption that whatever may be morally rotten in America, her foreign policy is sound. A somewhat chauvinistic militarism is common among Moral Majority supporters and leaders.

What prospects does Hunter hold out for American evangelicalism? He believes them to be 'less than cheerful'. Over time, evangelicalism has slidden from cultural dominance to structural insignificance. Cognitive bargaining with the dominant world-view leads to accommodation and, Hunter insists, compromise. Civility, subjectivity, narcissism and hedonism were not the traits of pioneer Puritanism! Admittedly, the perceived threat of the new class with its Romantic relativism has spurred to action a novel political movement. The effects of this have yet to be gauged, but Hunter thinks that overall modernity is too strongly established to permit real damage to the centre; peripheral persistence is the best that can be hoped for.

As for Britain, her conservative Protestants 'survive' secularization through internal strength and self-perpetuation. That, at least, is how Steve Bruce sees it. He notes the proliferation of premature obituaries to conservative Protestantism, especially after the Second World War. But neither the birth of the World Council of Churches nor the 'death of God' theologians has inhibited conservative Protestantism. Indeed, some would-be obituary writers have themselves begun to experience if not terminal decline at least dormancy. Conservative religion lives on. The reasons? One, that conservative Protestantism 'fits' with the modern world in several significant respects. Two, that conservative Protestants build a web of supporting institutions to sustain the *alternative* social milieux within which they live and move and have their being.

As to the 'fit' or accommodation to the modern world, Bruce sees common ground in the insistence on rationality. 'Thus, provided the believer can neutralize actual propositions that conflict with his beliefs, he can continue to work within a scientific world-view, as the large number of English evangelicals to be found in medicine and natural science demonstrates' (1984, p. 205). 'Fit' with modernity is also yielded by Protestant concern with individuals. The marginalizing and privatizing of faith in today's society presents no big hurdle for them: individual and family are areas where they feel most comfortable. (The rise of right-wing political individualism may also increase conservative Protestant credibility, in this view.) Further, the general cultural mood of pessimism resonates well with Protestantism, says Bruce. 'In a world of nuclear weapons, apparently uncontrollable economies, pollution and terrorism, the notion that man is innately sinful has considerable appeal' (1984, p. 205). Needless to say, conservative Protestants themselves may well reply that, *contra* Bruce, 'pessimism' is more properly rendered 'realism'. However, if his overall impression is of a Christianity obsessed with gloom and doom, then Christians, who lay great store by their 'blessed hope', would be right to feel chastened.

As to the alternative social *milieux* created by conservative Protestants, Bruce has in mind the fact that, even if they do not work within 'Christian' organizations, they may still spend most of their leisure time in church-related activities. With forgivable hyperbole, Bruce comes close to the bone:

> There are conservative Protestant holiday camps, tours of the Holy Land, boarding houses for born-again travelling salesmen, insurance policies for total abstainers, and an array of Bible study courses to match secular further education. Instead of *Time,* the conservative Protestant can read *Family* or *Today.* Instead of secular rock music, there is Gospel rock. For live entertainment there are crusades. In brief, while the liberal Protestant attempts to minimize that which separates the faith from the secular world, the conservative erects barriers (1983, p. 465).

Bruce says—and some of this is controversial—that because conservative Protestants gain little by way of new members via conversions of unchurched people, the explanation for their growth must lie in a superior ability to pass on belief and practice to the next generation. (Most evangelicals (56.7 per cent) claim to have been converted between ages twelve and twenty; only 12.8 per cent by means of a professional evangelist (Evangelical Alliance, 1968).)

Definitional difficulties bedevil studies such as Bruce's and Hunter's, and they freely admit this. Accuracy is sometimes sacrificed to neatness, however. Extreme examples, quoted to highlight the argument, end by being more memorable than the mundane averages.

Bruce's conservative Protestants are somewhat top-heavily 'fundamentalist' (perhaps because most of his research has been carried out in Scotland and Ulster) which means that, for instance, burgeoning Anglican evangelicalism receives short shrift. Hunter on the other hand flips between two different kinds of definition of evangelical. One is the pollsters' evangelical, who must of course be neatly pigeonholed. The pollsters' evangelicals account for a quarter of the total American population! Again, it is partly a question of region: rural folk evangelicalism of the southern states would be included in the pollsters' returns, but would probably never have heard of the books whose readership Hunter *also* describes as 'evangelical'. (In any case, the polls suggest that 37 per cent of their evangelicals have an incomplete high school education, not a group one would instinctively associate with reading (Marsden, 1984).) Such book readers would be among the 'other' kind of evangelical, who have specific affiliations to church and para-church groups and leaders.

Despite the excellent analyses of contemporary 'conservative Protestant' persistence, then, one is left with a slightly uneasy feeling that Berger's 'deadly dilemma' may not be the last word on strategies facing such churches towards the end of the twentieth century. At no point does Bruce or Hunter lower the tone of his studies to the level of the crude secularization story, which sees no place for Christianity in the modern world. But the residue of that tawdry tale may yet be rendering our understanding opaque.

A Missing Dimension?

It is clear that (as with all ideal types and models), the notions of accommodation and resistance do not conform precisely to any phenomena observable in the real world. They are not meant to. Rather, ideal types are fictions, constructed by the researcher as an aid to analysis. The accent is put artificially on a series of traits, isolated as pegs on which to hang empirical studies, and as standards by which to measure them. So ideal types are emphatically not 'ideals' (or the opposite!), and nor are they 'descriptions' of social reality. The ideal types of 'accommodation' or 'resistance' to secularization help us see a whole continuum of possible alternative postures in between the polar extremes. Moreover, they echo the biblical requirement that the Christian community negotiate the knife-edge 'in but not of the world'.

In Bruce's work on conservative Protestants in the UK, the social sources of expansion and strength may be traced to a *combination* of strategies. Such Christians both adjust their thinking to be in line with the world of science, without ever denying the reality of a realm beyond science (here is a form of accommodation), and at the same time maintain their supporting networks — from Christian rock music to Christian schools — which represents a mode of resistance. Even here lies a problem, however. When does 'accommodation' simply mean 'adaptation' (as in the radio advertisement I heard recently for a 'computer Bible school' run by the Salvation Army in Brampton, Ontario), and when does it mean 'assimilation' (as in the capitulation to a 'multi-faith' approach to Christian evangelism which accepts an 'other roads to God' line)?

Despite their usefulness in pinpointing the 'accommodating' tendencies of a denomination which permits the ordination of 'gay' clergy, or the 'resisting' parries of a church which clings tenaciously to an infallible Bible, one is left uneasy about the way these ideal types are sometimes used. Data may appear to be squeezed through these two filters in a rather contrived fashion. All too easily, by using words like 'options' and 'quandary', the ideal types sound as if they are actual choices confronting people. Worse, they may apparently be the *only* choices available: either the church is contemporary but compromised, or pure but passé. Here is an implicit assumption — perhaps only an impression — running through several secularization studies. But if it is present, as I suggest, then it may both distort the facts and discourage the faithful.

Since Berger's earlier writings (which is where the accommodation/resistance ideal types originated), he has gone some way towards correcting the initial impression that in today's Church one is more apt to encounter theological concessions to modern thought on the one hand, or the shoring up of sectarian defences, on the other, than steady earth-salting and Word-proclaiming or even Old-Testament-style social radicalism. But mileage is still made from these ideal types (or their equivalents) in such a way that the overall impression is that of a fragile future for the Church.

If Berger once contributed to that impression, then Bryan Wilson certainly still does (though this should not be taken as a denial of his frequently erudite insights into contemporary religion). By conceiving of religion as an agent of social control, which preserves the traditions of the past and only adjusts to the present when it seems inevitable for survival, he too misses any future-forging, prophetic movements within the Church. Or when they cannot escape his attention he downplays them as rhetorical flourishes or fads. Yet from the perspective of one prominent churchman (who is no naive believer in liberation theology's revolutionary aspirations, and yet refuses to write off that movement as mere faddishness) 'the prophetic element of the Jewish-Christian tradition is of peculiar importance for the renewal, and not just the maintenance, of society' (Preston, 1977, p. 71).

Of course, polarizations do exist in the Christian

community, and such divisions are a danger to the coherence of Christian mission. Although the association of 'conservative' theology and politics over against more 'radical' theology and politics appears to be somewhat dated today (which hangs another query over the 'deadly dilemma'), such splits are still apparent *within* specific folds. As far as evangelicals are concerned, one 'danger to mission' is that political criteria blinker biblical study, as when 'conservatives' find only 'creation ethics' and 'radicals' only 'kingdom ethics', which amounts to a tacit denial of the potentially unifying basic belief in the authority of the *whole* Bible. Needless to say, the time and place of biblical study always affect interpretation, and a sociology of theology can help to illuminate this process. Problems arise from a lack of awareness of, or an unwillingness to recognize, this fact.

So polarities do exist in fact (and to the detriment of Christian practice). The 'deadly dilemma' may mislead by insinuating that only polarized choices are available to the churches in a secular context. On their own they may constrict us to a gratuitously negative vision of today's options. The impression may be given that no substantial middle way exists.

Take the evangelicals mentioned in that *New York Times* article. Without claiming that they are a massive social force in American society, it is correctly stated that 'they are strengthening their own institutions and making deep inroads into the 50-year liberal leadership of the major Protestant denominations'. These people who 'stress a personal commitment to Jesus, confidence in the Bible, and enthusiasm for spreading the word . . .' are 'equipped by education and outlook to bring the historic tenets of the Protestant faith to bear on twentieth century problems'.

Some sympathetic observers of this trend towards evangelical zeal, manifest *both* in 'soul-winning' *and* in concern over poverty or the arms race, hail it as a 'Third Great Awakening'. Such hopes may turn out to be exaggerated, but, seen through Hunter's lens, they are summarily dismissed as 'a virtual sociological, not to mention legal, impossibility under the present conditions of modernity'. Further, in case the point be missed, 'The traditions of secularism have become too deeply engrained in American culture and institutional structure to permit anything but, at best, a large-scale, private sphere renewal' (1983, p. 33).

Similar comments apply in the British context. While one will always be able to winkle out eccentric evangelicals who can date the Second Coming, who await spiritual guidance before deciding which socks to wear or who believe that hymn-singing is an unbiblical practice at the threshold of the slippery slope, there is little evidence that they are more than a tiny minority. While Bruce's view comes nowhere near such idiosyncrasy, one does not come away with an entirely balanced picture. Plenty of evangelicals, for example, are uncomfortable (for various reasons) with the whole concept of mass crusade evangelism, so that the actual proportion who treat it as 'live entertainment' would be minuscule.

Again, while Bruce rightly comments that evangelicals have a strong history of social involvement, contemporary political reformism seems not to have caught his eye. It is unfortunate that figures are unavailable for evangelical support of the Labour Party or the Social Democratic Party. But even without them, the activities of organizations like The Shaftesbury Project (for research and encouragement of socio-political involvement) and the Evangelical Coalition for Urban Mission (devoted to inner-city, ethnic minority and youth work) give the lie to any suggestion that all believers in the atonement are other-worldly escapists.

Having indulged in mild criticism of Hunter and Bruce, it ought to be said once more that their perspectives are valuable. American evangelicals could do far worse than read Hunter to discover what they are up against in the power corridors of 'secular humanism'. And their brothers and sisters on both sides of the Atlantic stand to suffer the consequences if they ignore Bruce's reminder that any 'bridge-building' to the 'world' may induce two-way traffic-flow.

The Clergy: an Endangered Species?

Bryan Wilson likens today's clergy to 'charcoal burners or alchemists in an age in which the processes in which they were engaged had been rendered obsolete, technically or intellectually' (1966, p. 98). And in book titles like *The Fate of the Anglican Clergy* one gets an immediate whiff of impending doom. The contents of Towler and Coxon's book confirm this first impression. They say that many bewildered wearers of the cloth, lacking inspiration on how to span the widening gap between their role and modern social life, 'just stand and, as it were, allow the waves of marginality to break over them' (1979, p. 54). How has this situation arisen?

Towler and Coxon blame 'three secularizations' for this dismal state of affairs. First, in pre-Tudor times, clergy were an estate of the realm, operating in many spheres of life, and were nationally influential. But during the Tudor period, their social reach was reduced, leaving them only with a firm hold on education. Second, until 1837, clergy still kept a foothold in the class structure, maintaining their balance by their landowning associations and educational influence. The Victorian secularization saw new forms of capitalist finance tip the balance of power away from the land, while new legislation prised education from their grasp. The Church of England was demoted to denominational status, and subordinated to society. The third, contemporary secularization is marked by further contraction, as the church is no longer in any sense a central voluntary organization, but rather subsists on the social fringe. If the clergy had an authentic place within the occupational structure, they do not now.

Of course, one might object that Anglicanism is a special case, not replicated in situations where, for instance, there has never been a national church. That accepted, the general picture of declining social status and shrinking scope for once-accepted 'ministries' is not inaccurate. It is a matter of degree.

How do the clergy respond to this threat to their traditional position? In another, this time interdenominational study of *Ministers, Clergy, and Priests* (Ranson *et al.*, 1977), we encounter the familiar choice: the guardians of the sacred either adopt a 'siege mentality' or they 'accommodate'. Given the financial stringency of today, the siege is less likely to succeed where a paid minister is concerned, so some attempt at 'relevance' is on the cards. Different churches respond differently.

Dutch Catholics, for instance, having lost their hold on education and welfare, consciously offered their services at other levels, in giving ethical leadership in society. Many American clergy have drifted towards counselling and therapeutic services, often as an integral part of their church-based work. In France the 'worker-priest' movement was inaugurated in an effort to form bridgeheads into an industrial milieu. In Britain, as in other countries, one-time clergy (or intending clergy) may be found in the professions once connected with the Church, teaching and welfare work.

One effect of the churches' rationalization process — becoming more bureaucratically organized — is that the 'professional' status of the clergy is disputed. (Bureaucratic workers are rule-bound, professionals are relatively autonomous and may consider that their work is 'service'.) The end result, according to one American commentator, is that ecclesiastical structures come to be viewed as merely instrumental, and not of divine origin (quoted in Ranson *et al.,* 1977). From the churches' point of view this is an insidious form of 'internal secularization'. Bureaucratic law precludes body-life. But it also begs other questions.

Only recently, since the founding of theological colleges and seminaries, have clergy acquired the 'professional' tag. But because they are not like other professions in having unique skills or competence, that puts them out in the cold, socially speaking. In a sense, they are not even an 'occupational group', for they have no monopoly of particular knowledge or skills. Little wonder so many clergy, lacking a sense of divine calling, or of the intrinsic worth of preaching and pastoral practice, seek their occupational identity in some more socially recognized sphere (Davis, 1983).

Little wonder, either, that the expressive revolution of the 1960s was so welcome to some. For it provided new non-bureaucratic opportunities for de-structured congregations and devolved leadership. Many clergy took the role of 'expressive professionals', encouraging their flocks to participate more in worship and leadership.

While such liberation may have New Testament precedent, and doubtless served to release many grateful folk from the dead hand of tradition, such moves also have potentially retrograde effects. The authority with which the preacher announces 'Thus says the Lord' is somewhat enfeebled if the seminar style is adopted for all occasions: 'and what do *you* think?'. Harry Blamires complains about the confusion contained in a 1960s' sermon which, in true Romantic vein, described phrases like 'the Bible says' as 'authoritarian'. Quite the opposite is the case, he says. It is the person who asserts his own opinion who is authoritarian: 'authority saves us from . . . authoritarianisms exercised by those who have the loudest voices, the strongest arms, or the most assertive egos' (1980, p. 73). If he is right, loss of authoritative proclamation of the Good News could result from this particular clerical response to secularization.

Unfortunately for the churches, divisions are likely to persist within secular, pluralist situations. The oft-mentioned gap between pulpit and pew is one, but this may be matched by another—that between theological education and pulpit practice. 'Professional training', especially that which takes place within the orbit of secular universities, seems increasingly distant from the realities of the local church. The pastors of flocks are caught with painful awkwardness in the binds of secularization. The temptations are tremendous, either to hole up in a fundamentalist bunker, or to become a clerical chameleon, blending innocuously with shifting secular surroundings, or even to fall back on 'experience' as a sure-but-subjective guide (see Berger, 1979). Unless the Christian Church catches a glimpse of herself in this kind of word-mirror, energies will continue to be dissipated in irrelevancies, and leadership will continue to be limp.

But the picture need not be one of unrelieved gloom. The marginalization of the clergy is not in itself a crisis for Christianity. If professionalism does wither, this could be the death-knell for abstract pulpit theobabble as well. The self-made gaps between pulpit and pew could be narrowed. And as for church organization, related trends could also ease bureaucratic strangulation. As Davis says, 'as far as it is possible to discern the trends, the future shape of industrial society is likely to include more space for part-time, shared and more informal occupations within a more complex employment structure' (1983), and this means that, in biblical language, different gifts within the Body of Christ may have greater scope for development. More flexibility, and more opportunities for active involvement of a larger proportion of believers would, in New Testament terms, be signs of strength, not weakness.

Secularization: Challenge or Threat?
Secularization is not in itself a threat to the survival of Christianity. Nevertheless, if the churches mentioned in this chapter—particularly the evangelical ones—are to retain their

relative doctrinal robustness and contemporary relevance, the challenges of secularization will have to be faced head-on. But not only those of secularization. The 'other' process, of sacralization, poses problems of its own. These latter difficulties tend to be underestimated by those whose lens focuses only on 'secular humanism' as the enemy, or secularization as the cause of current crises.

The challenges are manifold. Where it was once forthcoming, state aid has now dried up. The Church can no longer count on such temporal scaffolding. Then, those who 'trust in princes' never were the subject of biblical approval. This does mean, however, that modern sources of authority, especially science and law, are more likely to conflict with the authority of relevation. Embrace could turn to abrasion. But there again, apostolic warnings are apposite: the Church is not immune from trouble with the powers that be. Moreover, the same pluralism promotes other potential rivals to faith, each requiring relevant response.

The uncoupling of Church and society, along with the stranding of Christianity at the social margins, presents a huge challenge. Christian confidence can crumble when faith appears as the slightly outdated leisure-time pursuit of a minority, especially if it turns out that the institution has been venerated more than its God. The 'civility' which soft-pedals sin within a so-called permissive culture will soon be indistinguishable from polite paganism. The noble vision of creation transformed and an earth filled with the knowledge of God is vulnerable in a world whose merely temporal horizon is proclaimed in the media and by the practice of the powerful. The scope of Christian claims on the whole spectrum of life is shrivelled as soon as a relative autonomy is granted to politics, economics or technology. Once Christians succumb to the view that such spheres should operate only according to their own internal criteria, they have in fact surrendered to secularity themselves.

But that is only the start of the difficulties. As we have seen, 'secularity' is not religiously neutral. In the incorrigible human quest for meanings, 'secular', temporal realities take on a new significance. As is appropriate in the modern world, with its exaggerated split between public and private worlds, new sacred themes emerge which express that dichotomy. On the one hand, political and economic ideologies—from monetarism to Marxism—make inflated claims for themselves in the public sphere. On the other hand, a plethora of potent symbols—often canned for easy consumption—form the new private pantheon. Body, sex and family are important here, but so also are the media-wrapped goodies of sport and rock music.

This is where 'secularization' can be such a misleading concept. For in many ways we have exchanged the overarching 'sacred canopy' not for another umbrella-like awning of 'secularism', but for a whole assortment of awnings. A variety of possibilities will do the job. Either a new movement which bears enough traces of conventional faith for it readily to be recognized as 'religion'—such as the 'Unification Church' or 'Scientology'—or some novel sacred theme or symbol which attracts devoted attention and motivates action, from Luckmann's 'mobility ethos' to Ellul's 'technique'. It is within this pluralist context that the Church has to find its place in the late twentieth century. The very idea of 'uniqueness' of a religion is doubted, and although few dare to take a clear stand, many are in the mass of 'seekers' (as Campbell suggests).

In a sense, then, the modern Church finds itself facing multiple challenges. Secularization spells a new relationship with 'state' and 'science' in particular. But parallel processes simultaneously bring further challenges reminiscent of other phases of Jewish-Christian history. Today's pluralism revives memories (or it *should do*) of the diversity of deities available in the Roman world of the early Church. And the fact that this pluralism also includes the 'invisible religion' of assorted sacred themes calls to mind the idolatries which so frequently seduced Old Testament society.

But as we have stressed repeatedly, secularization is paradoxical and ambiguous. What used to be billed as the 'end of religion' (the breakdown of state/Church collusion) is, as David Martin reminds us, the very 'essence of Christianity'. So from the churches' viewpoint secularization offers fresh opportunities as well as critical challenges. Liberated from the somewhat dubious dependence on state support, the Christian Church once more has the chance to be distinctive in message and practice—and critical of the *status quo*. And just as Christianity was once said to have contributed to secularization by 'disenchanting' nature and opening up untrodden paths of scientific investigation, so today the new 'sacreds' of technology and the nation state invite contemporary iconoclasm.

While secularization does present peculiar threats, and while the modern situation does magnify the challenge in several ways simultaneously, we are really experiencing new twists for age-old problems. The whole sociological paraphernalia of 'accommodating' or 'resistance' is clearly anticipated in the New Testament injunction to be 'in but not of the world'. And whatever sociologists say, that involvement in the world was originally intended to have a permeating, and not just a preservative, effect. Hence the expression 'the salt of the earth'. Further, the truth of the message was to be tested in the crucible of real life, making the 'intellectual' and 'normative' dimensions inseparable. Social theorists may put asunder what has thus been joined, only at peril of misunderstanding the very dynamic of Christian religion.

The evidence for a resilient Christian presence in the modern world should stimulate a new confidence in the power of the old faith to transform both person and world. It also gives room for manoeuvre, freedom to experiment (for instance in church leadership) within the forms of faith 'once delivered to the saints'. At the same time, if Christians go 'beyond secularization' and acknowledge that modernity is midwife to several new social forms of religion, then clearly a rejuvenation of 'idolatry-critique' is called for. Which, in a sense, brings us full circle. 'Secularization' which has too often been wielded as a weapon against Christianity, may be used by Christianity to locate the real enemy.

8: Secularization and Beyond: The Aftermyth

The official view was
            Don't Panic.
You didn't stone the prophet.
You didn't even censor him.
You didn't put him in prison.
You just put him in perspective.

(from Steve Turner's poem, *The Prophet*)

One frustration often encountered by readers of 'sociological' books is this. The critical cutting edge of analysis is blunted by careful qualification. What was once a worry is dismissed as a false alarm: Don't Panic. For those who are concerned about secularization in society and in the Church the message of this book is *not* 'Peace, peace, where there is no peace'. Our task is not to lull people into a soporific sense of security with sociological reassurances. Rather, by investigating the diverse dimensions of the world uncovered by secularization studies, we can get a clearer perspective on our social and religious context. Far from defusing concern about secularization, my aim has been both to draw on current research which indicates more accurately what we mean by the term, and also to expose other trends—especially 'sacralization—which in the past have been obscured by 'secularization'.

In this chapter I summarize our discussion of 'secularization', and make a plea that secularization studies be complemented with 'cultural analysis'. We briefly rehearse reasons for rejecting the received secularization story, while also pointing to the lasting usefulness of the concept for guiding us to important issues for our understanding of religion and society. Following this, the remainder of the chapter is concerned with the implications for sociology, society and Christianity of rethinking secularization.

Rethinking Secularization
All workers have to check over the tools of their trade from

time to time. Wear and tear take their toll. But tools can also fail because of bad design. Concepts are the tools of the social analyst, and they also require periodic examination and overhaul. Social analysts attempt to help us better understand our social situation by pulling together in a systematic way the kind of knowledge and insights available to all in everyday life. By deliberately focusing on one aspect of social life — like the relation between religion and society — social analysis tries to throw light on what is happening around us. So it is of utmost importance, especially when social science terms like 'secular' are used in ordinary conversation, that the tools are appropriate for the job.

So what should we do with 'secularization'? It cannot be abandoned, not only because it is so securely embedded in popular and technical usage, but because it undoubtedly refers to certain social realities of great import. It has value as a 'problematic', a concept which flags a cluster of social processes which deserve exploration. Some crucial changes have occurred in the modern world — Christianity now has to justify itself intellectually over against 'science', and socially over against the secular state — and these issues may be considered under the 'secularization' rubric (but see Cox, 1984).

Within 'secularization', however, is a complex tissue of ambiguity and paradox, of variety and nuance. We have tried to document some of this in the foregoing pages, standing on the shoulders of several contemporary social analysts. So it does make a big difference that today we inhabit what is loosely called 'secular society', but it is imperative that we are clear what we mean when we use the word.

For 'secular society' is only one way of looking at things. 'Secularization', though a useful string bag to encompass some aspects of contemporary society, should never be treated as *the one* concept which orients us to understand religion in the modern world. If it is used thus, it simply becomes a barrier to adequate analysis. Thankfully, there is today far more scepticism than there was twenty years ago about secularization as a global catch-all.

So we also have to move beyond secularization as a simple blanket description of what has happened to the religious life of industrial societies. This involves an openness to what is today called 'cultural analysis'. Not the rarefied study of 'high culture', of fine arts and music (though art and music are far from insignificant), but of culture as a way of life, expressed in symbols. Among the symbols which are looked to for meaning and which help define the landmarks or boundaries of social life are those which we have described as having a 'sacred' status. So 'sacralization' is one of the tools which I suggest we must use alongside 'secularization'.

Just to take one example, think of the clock. Although the mechanical clock came first, it was a vital component of the nascent industrial capitalist system. Time became a commodity; clock-time was a measure of day-to-day activities as wages were geared to measured hours. For the employer, 'time was money', so it is not hard to see how it might become 'sacred'. The 'labour force' could be co-ordinated using the clock, which thus emerged for employees as the symbol of routine — frequently an empty routine, stripped of moral meaning and purpose (Giddens, 1981; Banks, 1983). The timepiece thus came to symbolize the boundary of routine, rational time. Beyond measured time is another world. For Thomas Mann's Hans Castorp (in *The Magic Mountain*), taking off his watch meant contact with the abyss, with eternity (Bernice Martin (1981) discusses this further). Today, the computer seems set to acquire a similar level of cultural significance as did the clock before it. It is already a symbol worthy of close scrutiny, rapidly becoming a metaphor for 'mind' (as the clock became a metaphor for a 'mechanical' universe, see Bolter, 1984).

Cultural analysis takes an interest in actual patterns of symbol and sentiment, in how people make sense of the world. Of particular significance are the boundaries — the rules and regulations, the events and expectations, which give order to social life, and which also shift, sometimes gradually, sometimes suddenly. Link this up with an observation of changes in religious institutions, and the picture of how secularization studies may dovetail with cultural analysis becomes clearer. If, for instance, as Jeffrey Cox proposes (1982), many Victorian church people distinguished little between Christianizing British society and civilizing British society, it becomes less surprising that education and welfare should retain the potent symbolism of social regenerators long after those 'civilizing agents' had shed their theological justification. The cultural meaning of these institutions relates closely to their intertwining with church religion a century ago.

What's Wrong with Secularization?

Let us quickly put behind us the key objections to 'secularization'. I am not pretending that these objections are new. As already mentioned, critics of secularization have been busy ever since David Martin launched his first broadside in 1965. But it is worth going over the objections, because all too often some of the old connotations lie not far below the surface of modern accounts of secularization. They are probably impossible to erase fully, but must be questioned if they appear as part of a taken-for-granted account of modern society.

Firstly, secularization is rooted in a dichotomous view of society: 'before and after' the arrival of industrial capitalism. This suggests that there is more difference than continuity between historical periods. Religion, as a socially significant aspect of feudal society, is thought to lose out in at least two ways. One, the institutions of religion are stripped of their former roles, especially education, welfare and legitimation. Two, formally rational criteria increasingly determine the shaping of social life. Cost-benefit analysis and traffic lights take over from considerations of justice, sacrifice or service. Or at least that is the drift of this 'cultural bathtub' approach.

This makes secularization studies rather short-sighted. On the one hand the dichotomous view obscures the continuities of religious and quasi-religious belief and practice. 'Subterranean theologies' do persist, however, as do the institutional representation of historic Christianity, the churches. The continued quest for meaning, identity and hope, seen in the everyday construction of 'symbolic universes', also tends to remain hidden when one's eyes are glued to the supposed corrosive of religion. One other effect of the 'dichotomous' view is that further changes and ongoing trends may not be noticed. If one thinks only of a movement from community to society, for instance, in which Christianity loses its hold as the parish system falls prey to urban sprawl, then world-wide movements such as empire and new communications, which also affect Christianity, may be missed.

Secondly, secularization is rooted in rationalism. This is

almost bound to be the case, given the historical links between 'Enlightenment' and secularization. But the myopia of rationalism takes on a more subtle complexion within secularization studies. For Weber, rationality can assume several forms, including forms which could also be described as 'religious'. Yet Weber also considered religion *irrational*, and as having shrinking scope in the modern world.

Mary Douglas is especially scathing of this Weberian view. Convinced that 'primitive' societies can be highly secular, she also suggests why modern societies might be highly religious. If tides and seasons are the mysterious forces which call forth awe and a search for security in pre-modern society, why should not the vagaries and impersonality of bureaucracies produce similar responses today (1982, p. 11)? But then, even theologians fall prey to rationalist delusions. Rudolf Bultmann apparently believed that traditional faith is impossible in an age of electricity.

Thirdly, secularization is rooted in evolutionism. The shift to modern society has frequently been conceived as social change proceeding along lines analogous to biological evolution. Societies are said progressively to adapt themselves to new environmental conditions. Bryan Wilson, for example, who writes in this vein, uses the broad sweep of evolution as the canvas on which details of specific religious—and post-religious—phenomena are painted. This means that secularization is often pictured as a one-way street, with no 'U-turns' allowed.

As soon as the language of evolution comes into play, however, mechanical images predominate. This leads to a minimizing both of the variety and uniqueness of patterns of change, and the possibility that some event or movement simply does not fit the overall picture. Secularization is not a one-way street: it is not a single-track road either. The part played by active, reflexive humans in constituting such social weave is consequently denied or ignored. Thus some secularization studies have simply discounted the role of groups or individuals in actively attempting to determine the sacred/secular boundary lines.

Fourthly, secularization is rooted in reductionism. Religion turns out to be 'nothing but' a social (epi-) phenomenon. It is analytically reduced to one or two of its dimensions, and then assumed merely to be 'an agent of social control' or a 'projection'. This relates to the three previous critical points just made. With the coming of 'rational society', the onset of 'modernity', the prognosis for religion is poor. Within the evolutionary process it could well become extinct.

At this point, the sceptical social science consumer would be justified in asking how exactly the persistence, revival, new outbreaks, novel movements and public manifestations and private testimony of religion square with such a reductionist view. No one denies that religion may at times be manipulated by the state to obtain some desired end (the Romanian state uses the Orthodox Church in exactly this fashion to bolster national identity). Equally, religion may stimulate liberative activity: evangelical pressure against slavery was a vital contribution to emancipation last century, and analogous pressure is today exerted against *apartheid* and other oppressions in Africa and Latin America. But religion cannot logically be *reduced* to control agent—or to a mode of civil resistance. Reductionism is in the end self-contradictory. No single level of explanation can hope to deal in a final way with all religious phenomena.

What's Left of Secularization?
The above criticisms are by no means fatal to secularization studies. They do show, however, that great caution and a critical attitude are required. Secularization is usable as a problematic, a concept which points up significant aspects of modern society. It has no *explanatory* power in itself: only when used in conjunction with some other tools may it truly be illuminating.

Firstly, secularization points to a lack of public consensus on questions of truth and virtue. This does not mean that once-upon-a-time consensus existed. Rather, with the decline in direct social significance of the institutional churches, itself an aspect of the general 'uncoupling' of social spheres in the modern world, meanings have been cut loose from their original institutional homes. It cannot be taken for granted that anyone will agree on any specific matters of belief or morality. Quite the reverse: a remarkable plurality of such convictions—or lack thereof—characterizes societies within the Western ambit. This of course varies from society to society. The most obvious result is a widespread uncertainty about 'authority' and 'identity', which is manifest for instance in 'crises of political legitimation' and the 'quest for self-understanding', self-actualization, and so on. In other words, 'secularization' reminds us of the link between a loss of meaning which was once supplied in part by conventional religion, and some of the central social questions of our day.

Closely connected with this is the issue of the relation between Church and state. A palpable feature of the modern world is that religion has to justify itself without state aid. So the second set of relationships which 'secularization' invites us to investigate is that which obtains between religion and the 'powers that be'. Again this releases the concept from any involvement in the provision of blanket explanations. Rather, as David Martin masterfully demonstrates, the varied spectrum of possible patterns of secularization may be examined in a manner which deflates precisely that lust for uniform explanation.

A third area left standing after the removal of dangerously fragile elements of secularization studies is 'boundary definition'. That is to say, 'secularization' may be viewed as an ongoing social process in which groups and individuals are actively engaged in struggling to define the boundary between 'sacred' and 'secular'. Again, it defuses any notion of pre-set patterns of events which would culminate in the final social obliteration of religion. Battles over evolution or abortion may thus be seen as 'secularization contests', with no predetermined outcome. Of course, this also leads beyond conventional definitions of religion. It raises for example the question of how 'religious' is 'civil religion', and the means by which religion or the sacred is relocated in the contemporary context.

Fourthly, 'secularization' may find a role in highlighting 'temporal' preoccupation in a given social setting. Larry Shiner rightly notes that many use 'secularization' to denote a 'this-worldly' concern. The roots of secularization do include this dimension, which involves the outlawing of a transcendent dimension to human life and a preoccupation with temporal concerns (see Fenn, 1982, especially chapter 1). This resonates, biblically, with the burden of Ecclesiastes. Life 'under the sun' is life denuded of any purpose from the beyond the temporal horizon. Lacking a divine dimension, it constitutes the stifling and gloomy 'world without windows' (see further, Guinness, 1983, p. 57). Of course, if 'religion' were defined more broadly, one might also discover ways in which the temporal was socially invested with 'transcendent' qualities, a nuance missed by those who prefer to stick with the narrower definition.

Secularization Sociology and Beyond

Until the 1970s, secularization was frequently taken for granted within sociology. Even today it is still used uncritically by some, especially those outside the sociology of religion. I am not saying that secularization is capable of simple definition, which has been missed by these folk. No, the paradox and ambiguity embedded in secularization will remain as long as the field is studied: it is part of what secularization is all about. (In fact, like the best sociological concepts, it accurately captures some of the ambiguity and paradox which is an inescapable feature of human life.) The point is that, if today's society is accurately to be understood, the limitations and ambiguities of any concept must be made plain.

Much trouble could be avoided if the advice of treating secularization as a 'sensitizing concept' or 'problematic' were heeded. It cannot aspire to the status of social explanation, let alone a universal or evolutionary explanation. It is an archaeologist's flag, indicating an important site worthy of careful investigation. It even leads us to ask some appropriate questions, but cannot in itself give the answers. It is not the explanation so much as the thing to be explained.

It is unfortunate that the sociology of religion developed as a separate sub-discipline within social analysis and theory. Of course religion deserves attention in its own right. But the effect of this intellectual division of labour has been to insulate 'mainstream' sociology from 'religious' concerns, to the detriment of both. (A similar division of labour has distanced 'historical explanation' from religion.) David Martin's achievement in marrying political sociology with sociology of religion, and Bryan Turner's efforts to relate 'materialist' (that is, to do with the body) explanations to religion should encourage a new *rapprochement,* which is long overdue.

For the classical sociologists, religion was a central aspect of social explanation. Christianity in particular was deeply implicated in the very emergence of the modern world. Noting the threats to religious institutions and practices in the modern world, they each asked their own version of the question, 'after religion, what then?'. Perhaps they were already making some unwarranted or premature assumptions about the imminent demise of Christianity. But they at least recognized the significance both of Christianity's role in the development of the West, and of the kinds of questions associated with Christianity which still demanded answers even in a 'post-Christian' society.

We could do worse today than to follow classical sociology's emphasis on religion within general social explanation. (In fact, the growing interest in 'cultural analysis' reflects just such a concern, in my opinion.) 'Secularization' would continue to signal, among other things, the loss of legitimation experienced by the churches in the modern world, and the way legitimation is sought with reference to the state or to science. But the spotlight would be on the *continuity* of appeal to symbols to make sense of reality and to respond emotionally and ethically to it. We could do worse, then, than return to some classical sociologists' *aims,* while happily jettisoning some of their *assumptions.*

Within the 'cultural analysis' framework (see Wuthnow *et al.,* 1984), space is made both for exploring the social consequences of diminishing public appeal to and support for conventional religion, and for discovering what new social forms of religion may be emerging today. This does not spell some metatheoretical reconciliation between Bryan Wilson and Thomas Luckmann, but it does mean that each of their contributions to secularization studies should be taken seriously. The grounds of Wilson's dismissal of Luckmann certainly appear shaky in this light.

From this starting point, the newly significant religious and cultural symbols of our day may be examined. There is a considerable literature of debate over this, one prominent theme of which is the idea of 'autonomy'. It could be argued for instance that autonomy is a key aspect of the 'sacred' of the contemporary world, and that this may be illustrated in both public and private realms. In public, an ideology like nationalism may betray its rootedness in a 'sacred' desire for autonomy. This would dovetail with the proposal made by Anthony Giddens (which makes no pretence at being 'sociology of religion'), that nationalism be explained in terms of the insecurity of being human, felt in situations where other more traditional forms of legitimation have collapsed. In the private sphere, one again finds a focus on 'autonomy', this time in relation to 'sacred' themes of sexuality, self-realization, and so on. And once more, in 'autonomy', one hears the distant echo of biblical themes. Doing what was 'right in their own eyes' was the hallmark of ancient Israel's rejection of the divine dimension to life, as personified in the rule of the 'Judges'.

Moves such as this take us a long way beyond taken-for-granted notions of secularization. They invite scepticism about the solidity of 'secularization' as a basic for social explanation. Far better to think of secularization at least as being open to question, both on the basis of evidence of conventional religious reversals (the growth of Christianity in modernizing Africa, for instance) and on the basis of a cultural analysis which highlights the presence of new sacred themes within the ongoing human activity of symbol-making. Thus Robin Gill proposes an 'alternating model' of secularization (1975), and Martin Marty suggests a 'religio-secular model of indeterminacy' (1982). Such initiatives deserve support.

One last point. The critique of reductionism in respect of religion could facilitate a new recognition of the central place of religion in modern as well as in ancient societies. Take another area of social analysis beset by reductionism: the family. Mark Poster's *Critical Theory of the Family* explodes many reductionist fallacies, and he argues instead that the family be seen as 'its own centre of intelligibility' (1982). If religion were seen as its own centre of intelligibility, this would lead analysts to expect things—the development of civil religion perhaps?—which otherwise come as a surprise. A further consequence, as far as Christianity is concerned, is that its history could be seen as having its own integrity. From this viewpoint medieval Christendom could never qualify as a 'golden age' of faith.

Secular Society and Beyond

Modern society, seen through the lens of secularization, is in a state of flux. Not only has society split away from any close ties with institutional religion, and not only have the worlds of daily routine, government, commerce and the media been left without any semblance of agreed transcendent dimensions or moral meaning, modern society is even losing the vocabulary with which to discuss such matters. In many ways the fabric of our world is woven with the threads of a bureaucratic web, and public life is dominated by the rational criteria of efficiency and technique. The process of cutting loose 'meaning' from its older cultural carriers has had profound social consequences. I comment only on three.

Firstly, those two major challengers of conventional Christianity, science and the state, each find themselves in some disarray today. Having attempted to distance themselves from any context of metaphysical or religious commitment, they seem to have encountered some severe contradictions of attempted autonomy. In science, the elaborate edifice of foundationalism (the view that theory is built on indubitable 'facts') is exhibiting stress symptoms, with the result that urgent efforts are made both to shore it up and to replace it. In the case of the state, it is clear that the appeal to a divine law 'above' human laws has been all but forsaken. But the result has hardly been a steady rational trend towards agreement on the role and tasks of the state! Political expediency, and the power of ratings over party policy, is often the order of the day.

Closely related to this, secondly, is the ethical vacuum in more than one crucially important life-area. Alasdair MacIntyre expresses some of his fears for human life in *After Virtue* (1981). Some dismiss him as alarmist, while others acknowledge that his outlook resonates with what can be observed. You do not have to believe with him that we are entering a new 'dark age' to see that without some agreed desiderata for social virtue the prospects for civilized life on earth are somewhat bleak.

In regard to new technology, Hans Jonas has also raised an alarm (1984). He shows how present developments are proceeding largely without reference to ethical criteria. Yet if a craftsman—such as a blacksmith—required an ethic, how much more do we, whose technological decisions by contrast have such long-term and hard-to-reverse effects. Medical and bio-technology raises these questions acutely. Human life itself now appears to be manipulable in the cause of science and social engineering. As Oliver O'Donovan indicates, the potential 'crime against humanity' involved in embryo research is not necessarily the old-fashioned one of killing babies, 'but the new and subtle crime of making babies to be ambiguously human, of presenting to us members of our own species who are doubtfully proper objects of compassion and love' (1984, p. 65). It takes little imagination to see how 'ethical vacua' and 'dark ages' are related to secularization studies.

A third phenomenon which relates to secularization is that of insulating people (the technical term is 'sequestering') from life-crises, suffering and death. Societies have developed which increasingly leave the 'management' of the emotional life to 'expressive professionals', the psychiatrist and the social worker. Life-crises, which in more traditional societies are meshed into an overarching system of meaning (often religious in the formal sense) are now left in curious limbo. It is by no means clear that modern societies cope successfully with this vacuum of meaning. What is clear is the rising tide of felt need for emotional assistance in a world of family disintegration, loss of employment, and anxiety over threats of cancer, nuclear holocaust and, for many, hunger.

But if these are some areas negatively affected by changes relating in some ways to secularization, it must also be remembered that secularization does not tell the whole story. At a certain point, 'secularization' begins to blinker us. Even without the crude old tales of society having progressed beyond the religious stage of its evolution, we still hear of society being almost monolithically secular, having lost a feel for the religious and even the sacred dimensions of life. Such exaggerations befog our view of contemporary society.

Firstly, there does seem to be evidence of a quest for certainty and for 'answers'. The political swing from the mid-1970s in the North Atlantic region, towards fairly dogmatic views and policies, illustrates this. The success of a revived fundamentalism—most strikingly in the USA—also lends support to this view. The tolerance-level for uncertainty among the large majority in any society is probably fairly low. Until recently, the predominant liberal culture in North Atlantic societies has derided such inability to embrace relativism and ambiguity, making it hard to express straightforward beliefs and traditional dogma. But as Daniel Bell has put it (in a paper some of whose other theorems I doubt), 'The exhaustion of Modernism and the emptiness of contemporary culture mitigate that social pressure', allowing 'simple pieties' and 'direct homilies' to come to the fore

(1977, p. 444). Although nothing on the scale of the 'Moral Majority' is likely to wash onto British—still less French—shores, European societies do have some weak analogues of their own. They include minor moral crusades, Scandinavian Christian political options, and a growth in British Pentecostalism (not unassociated with ethnic minorities).

It may also be, secondly, that we can expect other 'returns of the sacred' to which Bell alludes in the same paper. One is the 'redemptive' search for 'community', or for 'mediating institutions' to bridge the perceived gap between deracinated individual and bureaucratic society. The other is a return to some mythic and mystical modes of thought. The influence of Eastern thought-forms could be decisive here. Such a quest for 'totality' or 'self-unification' may well become more urgent if the one-dimensionality of computer culture is felt as a serious threat.

The whole question of a 'crisis of secularity' or the 'exhaustion of Modernism' may well require much more serious examination than that accorded it thus far. Although there have always been pockets of resistance to modernity and secularity, as Peter Berger puts it, 'manifestations of counter-secularity in recent decades have been particularly vigorous' (Berger, 1983, p. 16). These include the burgeoning 'Third World' religious movements, the sturdy resilience of the churches in Eastern Europe, and two phenomena in the USA: the counter-culture and the renewal of conservative Protestantism.

But Berger's argument goes further than mere contraindications of vanishing religion. Secularity may be in trouble, he says, because of the outworking of its own doctrine of moral pluralism. By definition there can be no one definitive 'secular' approach to a given issue, and thus 'secularity' is unlikely, at least in the USA, to become monolithic. Cultural variations in secularization patterns being what they are, however, Berger admits that the situation in Scandinavia, for instance, is unlikely to mirror that in the USA.

If, then, we are to take seriously the study of society 'beyond secularization', we must look at all signs of a 'return of the sacred' and of a 'crisis of secularity'. But if going beyond secularization means the acceptance of a wider definition of religion, then we also have to take note of which cultural symbols are taking on a sacred significance.

Elsewhere, sexuality is seen as a prime candidate for just such an investigation. We have also noted the creation of the 'silicon idol'. This latter symbol has enjoyed a spectacular rise in devotion, both at the private shrine of the home micro (personal computer) and in the public faith put in information technology as a *sine qua non* of any future good life. The interplay between ideologies (such as progress through economic growth) and the hope invested in things like new technology deserves more than a cursory glance.

Christianity, Secularization and Beyond

Secularization is a valuable tool for assessing the state of Christianity in the late twentieth century. It can also be exaggerated, or seen in an exclusively negative light. This is why I have written of the 'myths' as well as the 'realities' of secularization. The Christian churches have the ticklish task of both getting to grips with the practical implications of secularization, and of liberating themselves from some of the inhibiting and negative connotations of secularization which are hidden within the myths.

Secularization opens our eyes to the cultural isolation of Christianity, the result of Church and society being progressively uncoupled. It draws attention to the so-called rationalization of public life, *and* the transfer of some calculating, quantitative, efficiency-obsessed methods right into the organizations of the Church. Not only does the qualitative, the affective, the concern with care and compassion either diminish in wider society or, in a pendulum swing, become an overriding priority, but such virtues may also become less visible within the Church.

Secularization is closely bound up with the same modern dynamic which splits our social *milieu* into public and private segments, leaving Christianity artificially grounded on the private shoreline. The coherence of Christian practice is corroded in this way. The public sphere drifts off on its own course (Christian participants in it having to follow that course in order to survive) and the private sphere comes to be seen as the 'natural' (and secure) locus of religion, in family and leisure time. This private space is, however, invaded by hosts of other options, as society becomes increasingly pluralistic. Christianity faces strong competition, from both overtly and implicitly religious quarters.

Added to all this is the sheer difficulty, in a 'secular' context, of translating Christian truth into modern terms. Memories of 'Christendom' (at least in Europe) are now so badly faded that Christians are obliged to start from scratch in explaining the Good News. Common or customary religion, with its residue of Christian motifs, persists, but probably muddies more than it clarifies the waters. Myriad messages from the media and from other sacred alternatives serve only to distort things further. The historical reality of Jesus Christ is hard to rescue from use of the name either as an expletive, a charm, or on a similar level to Santa Claus.

At the same time, the churches overlook one of the *myths* of secularization at their peril. For the competition faced within the pluralist context is not only from the state, or new religious movements, but from new sacred areas which crystallize as centres of meaning and devotion. The cruder secularization story fails to expose these realities. And yet the appearance of such 'invisible religion' should be anticipated by those long-accustomed to hearing prophetic denunciations of idolatry, which in New Testament times is extended explicitly to items such as uncontrolled sexual appetites and conspicuous consumption. The rediscovery of these themes gives scope for considerable cross-fertilization of sociological and theological modes of understanding.

Secularization does create its own dangers for the churches. In the context just outlined, one trap is to make new alliances in an age when state support is absent, The 'new right' currently represents one potential partner, some varieties of 'liberation theology', another. Such polarizations are damaging to the Christian cause, and the only long-term antidote to them is to find modes of reconciliation which retain their Christian integrity.

The churches should not allow themselves to be misled by another secularization myth, however, which is that damaging polarizations are the only future facing them. The 'accommodate or resist' duo, if misconstrued as a real choice, rather than just an extreme way of highlighting modern tensions, can yield a deeply negative impression. Either faith is diluted through compromise or retreats to the fortress and raises the drawbridge. Christianity either loses its uniqueness and distinctiveness, or its relevance and applicability. There is no sociological or other evidence that the extremes are unavoidable. In real life, the churches have to find a passage through the world which adapts faith to time and place without sacrificing its fundamental integrity.

Another danger is the implicit acceptance by Christians of the secular doctrine that the Church merely offers an obscure minority option. This comes to light every time that an 'expert' such as a doctor is assumed to have 'sufficient reason' for a particular viewpoint or decision. A division of labour develops in which Christians may only speak of prescribed 'spiritual' matters; never on science, politics or medicine. While the world would be better off without naive and ignorant pronouncements by religious pundits, to allow Christian voices to be gagged in such matters is to fly in the face of the biblical directive to be Christian in *all* spheres of life. Without a contemporary Christian presence, participating in the diverse worlds of homemaking or information technology, Christian witness will be inadequate, and the cultural marginality of Christianity will simply be reinforced.

A third danger is that of underplaying the importance of belief. From outside the Church, popular psychological attempts to explain away belief, and from within the Church, a subjective and experience-centred 'faith' unintentionally conspire together to sap the solidities of biblical belief. But beliefs are not mere social epiphenomena, the surface manifestation of other realities. Current social scientific attention paid to 'ideology' demonstrates that this is not an outworn concern. Yet some Christians seem vulnerable to seduction at this point, downplaying 'doctrine' and 'word' in favour of voguish activism or ecstasis. Durkheim and Weber, in their respective sociologies of religion at least grasped the tremendous power of belief in society. Today's evidence does not suggest that this has waned. Bruce, for instance, argues that the strength of 'conservative Protestantism' is closely tied up with its distinctive beliefs.

For Christianity is not doomed, as the myth of secularization hints, when deprived of its supposed capacity to act as a sort of social cement. The fact that Christianity has historically contributed to social stability, justice and harmony at certain moments does not mean that this is its intended central purpose. Even though Christian failure to seek justice, peace and so on, is just that—Christian failure—this still does not touch the essence of faith. Christianity has persisted through centuries of opposition and extreme marginality, as well as through centuries when it had 'official religion' status. Eleven at-first-bewildered disciples preaching repentance to suspicious Jews within the hostile environment of imperial Rome was, after all, where things began.

Secularization also offers new opportunities. The uncoupling process which now enables the Church to operate without the dubious benefit of state assistance defines more exactly the boundaries between Church and world. The situation in more than one country now more nearly resembles that of the first-century Church. The Christian community may authentically take on some 'counter-cultural' qualities, rather than naively defending the *status quo*. The revival of some 'Anabaptist' emphases, especially in relation to 'simple lifestyle', Third World concern and rejection of material progress via economic growth is no coincidence.

Although no one can predict whether any aspects of a Christian outlook will be able to penetrate the centres of 'public' life, from a sociological viewpoint the fact that other—sometimes less desirable—'counter-cultural' motifs have found a foothold there suggests that opportunities may be available. Christian faithfulness at any rate demands that some attempt be made. Our forebears, exiled in Babylon, also faced formidable obstacles in seeking 'peace and prosperity' in a city whose name was a byword for hostility to YHWH.

The existence of opportunities is highlighted by the 'secularity crisis'. Today's ecological, political, nuclear and life dilemmas cry out for wisdom from beyond the merely temporal horizon. Without contributing to the mood of cultural pessimism, the churches could draw on the rich resources of a text such as Ecclesiastes, which puts its proverbial finger on the futility of all 'autonomous' schemes for self-redemption. In the same spirit, the chance is here for the churches to speak into current crises with the essential Christian gospel of forgiveness through Christ and hope in the act of 'remembering your Creator'.

We are left, then, with an elusive, enigmatic, paradoxical and ambiguous concept. 'Secularization' is a vital tool for the churches' self-understanding at the eve of the third millennium. But its perverse myths as well as its profound realities must be taken into account by all who would use it. The social situations illuminated by studies of the secular and the sacred offer both obstacles and opportunities for contemporary Christianity.

At the same time, the social and the cultural are only two dimensions of our whole human lives. While I have endeavoured to show that sociology need not itself be secular, or a vehicle of secularization (in the sense of shutting us up to a temporal horizon), it can still only throw light on part, not the whole. And even the whole, Christians confess, is only seen through a glass, darkly.

Social analysis, properly conceived, and without the millstone of 'methodological atheism', should enable us to have a clearer picture of the real social world, such that we are freed to act in it with greater consistency and less bad faith. For sociology—including the concept of secularization! —is less of a threat to faith than it is a challenge to Christian practice.

Bibliography

Abrams, Philip, and McCulloch, Andrew,
1976 *Communes, Sociology, and Society.* Cambridge, Cambridge University Press.
Abrams, Philip,
1982 *Historical Sociology.* Shepton Mallet, Open Books.
Acquaviva, Sabino,
1979 *The Decline of the Sacred in Industrial Society.* Oxford, Blackwell.
Anthony, Dick, and Robbins, Thomas,
1982 'Contemporary Religious Ferment and Moral Ambiguity', in Barker, ed., 1982 q.v.
Ausmus, Harry,
1982 *The Polite Escape: on the Myth of Secularization.* Athens, Ohio University Press.
Banks, Olive,
1981 *The Faces of Feminism.* London, Martin Robertson.
Barker, Eileen,
1984 *The Making of a Moonie.* Oxford, Blackwell.
1982 ed., *New Religious Movements: a Perspective for Understanding Society.* New York, Edwin Mellen.
1980 'Science and Theology: Diverse Resolutions of an Interdisciplinary Gap by the New Priesthood of Science' (*Interdisciplinary Science Reviews*, 5, 4).
Bebbington, David,
1982 *The Non-conformist Conscience.* London, Allen and Unwin.
1984 'Evangelicals and the Role of Women 1800—1930' (*Christian Arena*, December) pp. 19—23.
Bell, Daniel,
1977 'The Return of the Sacred: the Argument on the Future of Religion' (*British Journal of Sociology*, 28, 4) pp. 419—49.
1976 *The Cultural Contradictions of Capitalism.* New York, Basic Books.
Bellah, Robert,
1970 *Beyond Belief.* New York, Harper and Row.
Berger, Peter,
1983 'From the Crisis of Religion to the Crisis of Secularity', in Mary Douglas and Stephen Tipton, eds, *Religion and America: Spirituality in a Secular Age.* Boston, Beacon Press.

1979 *The Heretical Imperative.* New York, Anchor—Doubleday.

1977 *Pyramids of Sacrifice.* New York, Anchor—Doubleday.

1974 (and others) *The Homeless Mind.* Harmondsworth, Penguin.

1969 *The Sacred Canopy.* New York, Anchor—Doubleday, *The Social Reality of Religion.* Harmondsworth, Penguin.

Berlin, Isaiah,

1956 *The Age of Enlightenment.* New York, Mentor.

Frederick Bird,

1976 'A Sociological Analysis of New Religious and Para-religious Movements'. In Crysdale and Wheatcroft, eds. 1976 q.v.

Birnbaum, Norman, and Lenzer, Gerhardt,

1969 *The Sociology of Religion.* Englewood Cliffs, NJ, Prentice-Hall.

Blamires, Harry,

1980 *Where Do We Stand?.* Ann Arbor, Servant.

1963 *The Christian Mind.* London, SPCK.

Bocock, Robert,

1974 *Ritual in Industrial Society.* London, Allen and Unwin.

Bolle, K. W.

1970 'Secularization as a Problem for the History of Religion' (*Comparative Studies in History and Society,* 12, 3) pp. 242—59.

Bolter, David,

1984 *Turing's Man: Western Culture in the Computer Age.* Chapel Hill, University of North Carolina Press, and London, Duckworth.

Brierley, Peter,

1982 *UK Christian Handbook.* London, Evangelical Alliance/ Bible Society.

Bruce, Steve,

1984 *Firm in the Faith.* Aldershot, Gower.

1984a *One Nation Under God?* Belfast, Queen's University Dept. of Social Studies.

1983 'The Persistence of Religion: Conservative Protestantism in the UK' (*Sociological Review,* 31, 3) pp. 453—70.

Budd, Susan,

1979 *Varieties of Unbelief.* London, Heinemann.

1973 *Sociologists and Religion.* London, Collier-Macmillan.

Burrow, John,

1966 *Evolution and Society.* Cambridge, Cambridge University Press.

Campbell, Colin,

1982 'New Religious Movements, the New Spirituality, and Post-industrial Society', in Eileen Barker, ed., 1982, q.v.

1971 *Towards a Sociology of Irreligion.* London, Macmillan.

Caplow, Theodore,
1984 'Looking for Secularization in Middletown', in Patrick MacNamara, ed., *Religion: North American Style*. Belmont, Ca, Wordsworth.

Chadwick, Owen,
1975 *The Secularization of the European Mind in the Nineteenth Century*. Cambridge, Cambridge University Press.

Clark, David,
1982 *Between Pulpit and Pew*. Cambridge, Cambridge University Press.

Cox, Jeffrey,
1982 *The English Churches in a Secular Society*. Oxford, Oxford University Press.
1984 'Is Secularization a Useful Concept? No, not even in Twentieth-century Britain', Paper read at Southern Conference on British Studies.

Crysdale, Stewart, and Wheatcroft, Les,
1976 *Religion in Canadian Society*. Toronto, Macmillan.

Currie, Robert, Gilbert, Alan, and Horsley, L.,
1977 *Churches and Churchgoers: Patterns of Church Growth in the British Isles since 1700*. Oxford, Oxford University Press.

Davis, Howard,
1983 'A Sociological Perspective on Anglican Ministry' (*Proceedings of Anglican Evangelical Assembly*).

Davis, Kingsley,
1948 *Human Society*. New York, Macmillan.

Dekker, Gerard,
1978 'The Relation between Sociology and Theology', Paper read at Blackfriars Symposium on Sociology and Theology, Oxford.

Dobbelaere, Karel,
1984 'Secularization Theories and Sociological Paradigms: Convergences and Divergences' (*Social Compass*, XXXI, 2–3) pp. 199–219.
1981 *Secularization: a Multi-dimensional Concept*. (Current Sociology Monograph, 29, 2).

Douglas, Mary,
1982 'The Effects of Modernization on Religion' (*Daedalus, Winter*).

Durkheim, Emile,
1958 *Socialism and Saint-Simon*. Alvin Gouldner, ed., London, Routledge and Kegan Paul.

Elias, Norbert,
1978 *The Civilizing Process*. Oxford, Blackwell.

Ellul, Jacques,
1976 *The New Demons*. Oxford, Mowbrays.
1964 *The Technological Society*. New York, Vintage.

Evangelical Alliance,
1968 *Background to the Task.* London, Evangelical Alliance/ Scripture Union.
Fenn, Richard,
1982 *Liturgies and Trials: the Secularization of Religious Language.* Oxford, Blackwell.
1978 *Toward a Theory of Secularization.* Storrs, Conn., *Journal for the Scientific Study of Religion* Monograph.
Foucault, Michel,
1978 *The History of Sexuality.* New York, Random House.
Geertz, Clifford,
1966 'Religion as a Cultural System', in Michael Banton, ed., *Anthropological Approaches to the Study of Religion.* London, Tavistock.
Gellner, Ernest,
1974 *The Legitimation of Belief.* Cambridge, Cambridge University Press.
Gerth, Hans, and Mills, C. Wright,
1958 *From Max Weber.* New York, Oxford University Press.
Giddens, Anthony,
1985 *The Constitution of Society.* Cambridge, Polity Press.
1979 *Central problems in Social Theory.* London, Macmillan.
1972 *Emile Durkheim: Selected Writings.* Cambridge, Cambridge University Press.
Gilbert, Alan,
1980 *The Making of Post-Christian Britain: a History of the Secularization of Modern Society.* London, Longmans.
Gill, Robin,
1975 *The Social Context of Theology.* Oxford, Mowbrays.
Glasner, Peter,
1977 *The Sociology of Secularization: the Critique of a Concept.* London, Routledge and Kegan Paul.
Goodridge, Martin,
1983 'Managers as Secular Practitioners', Paper read at CISR Conference, London.
1975 'Ages of Faith: Romance or Reality?' (*Sociological Review,* 23, 2) pp. 381–96.
Goudzwaard, Bob,
1984 *Idols of Our Time.* Leicester and Downers Grove, Il, Inter-Varsity Press.
Gouldner, Alvin,
1976 *The Dialectic of Ideology and Technology,* London, Macmillan.
Greeley, Andrew,
1972 *The Persistence of Religion.* London, SCM Press, *Unsecular Man.* New York, Dell.

Guinness, Os,
1983 *The Gravedigger File.* London, Hodder and Stoughton.
Habermas, Jurgen,
1976 *Legitimation Crisis.* London, Heinemann.
Hackett, Rosalind,
1983 'Secular Wheat and Religious Chaff: the Emergence of Nigerian Civil Religion', Paper read at CISR Conference, London.
Hammond, Philip,
1969 'Peter Berger's Sociology of Religion: an Appraisal' (*Soundings,* 52) pp. 415ff.
Harrison, Beverly Wildung,
1975 'The Early Feminists and the Clergy: a Case-study in the Dynamics of Secularization' (*Review and Expositor,* 72, Winter).
Hobsbawm, Eric,
1962 *The Age of Revolution: Europe 1789—1848,* London Weidenfeld and Nicholson.
Hoge, Dean, and Roozen, D. A.,
1979 *Understanding Church Growth and Decline 1950—1978.* New York, Pilgrim Press.
Hunter, James Davison,
1983 *American Evangelicalism: Conservative Religion in the Quandary of Modernity.* Newark, NJ, Rutgers University Press.
Jonas, Hans,
1984 *The Imperative of Responsibility.* Oxford, Oxford University Press.
Keyes, Dick,
1984 *Beyond Identity.* Ann Arbor, Servant.
Kumar, Krishan,
1978 *Prophecy and Progress.* Harmondsworth, Penguin.
Ladurie, Emmanual LeRoy,
1980 *Montaillou.* Harmondsworth, Penguin.
Lane, Christel,
1982 'The New Religious Life in the Soviet Union: How and Why does it Differ?' (*International Journal of Sociology and Social Policy*) pp. 44—57.
Lemert, Charles,
1979 'Science, Religion, and Secularization' (*Sociological Quarterly,* 20) pp. 445—61.
Lovejoy, Arthur,
1960 *The Great Chain of Being.* New York, Harper and Row.
Luckmann, Thomas,
1977 'Theories of Religion and Social Change' (*Annual Review of the Social Sciences of Religion,* 1) pp. 1—28.
1976 'A Critical Rejoinder' (to Bryan Wilson) (*Japanese Journal of Religious Studies,* 3—4, December) pp. 277—9.

1967 *The Invisible Religion.* London, Collier-Macmillan.
Lyon, David,
1985 'Rethinking Secularization: Retrospect and Prospect' (*Review of Religious Research*, 26, 3, March) pp. 228—43.
1984 'Secularization: the Fate of Faith in Modern Society?' (*Themelios*, September) pp. 16—22.
1983 *Sociology and the Human Image.* Leicester and Downers Grove, Il, Inter-Varsity Press.
1983a 'Sociology and Humanness: the Action-Structure Tension in Secular and Christian Thought' (*Sociologia Internationalis*, 21, 1—2) pp. 51—68.
1983b 'Valuing in Social Theory: Post-Empiricism and Christian Responses' (*Christian Scholars' Review*, XII, 4) pp. 324—38.
1981 'Secularization and Sociology: the History of an idea' (*Fides et Historia*, XII, 2) pp. 38—52.
MacIntyre, Alasdair,
1981 *After Virtue.* London, Duckworth.
1967 *Secularization and Moral Change.* Oxford, Oxford University Press.
McKown, Delos,
1981 'Contemporary Religion Versus Science' (*Chemtech*, June).
McLeod, Hugh,
1982 *Religion and the People of Western Europe.* Oxford, Oxford University Press.
1980 'The Dechristianization of the Working Class in Western Europe: 1850—1900' (*Social Compass*, 27, 2—3) pp. 191ff.
MacRae, Donald,
1974 *Max Weber.* London, Fontana.
McSweeney, Bill,
1980 *Roman Catholicism: the Search for Relevance.* Oxford, Blackwell.
Marsden, George,
1984 'Evangelicalism in the Sociological Laboratory' (*Reformed Journal*, June).
1983 'America's "Christian Origins": Puritan New England as a Case-study', in Stanford Reid, ed., *The Influence of John Calvin on History.* Grand Rapids, Zondervan.
1980 *Fundamentalism and American Culture.* New York and Oxford, Oxford University Press.
Martin, Bernice,
1981 *A Sociology of Contemporary Cultural Change.* Oxford, Blackwell.
Martin, David,
1979 'General Tendencies and Historical Filters' (*Annual Review of the Social Sciences of Religion*).
1978 *A General Theory of Secularization.* Oxford, Blackwell.

1978 *The Dilemmas of Contemporary Religion*. Oxford, Blackwell.
1969 *The Religious and the Secular*. London, Routledge and Kegan Paul.
1965 'Towards Eliminating the Concept of Secularization', in Julius Gould, ed., *The Penguin Survey of the Social Sciences*. Harmondsworth, Penguin.
Marty, Martin,
1982 'Religion in American since Mid-Century' (*Daedalus*, Winter) pp. 149—63.
1969 *The Modern Schism: Three Paths to the Secular*. New York, Harper and Row.
Marwick, Arthur,
1982 *British Society since 1945*. Harmondsworth, Penguin.
Marx, Karl, and Engels, Friedrich,
1967 *The Communist Manifesto* (Introduction by Taylor, A. J. P.), Harmondsworth, Penguin.
Mehl, Roger,
1970 *The Sociology of Protestantism*. London, SCM Press.
Mouw, Richard,
1981 'Assessing the Moral Majority' (*The Reformed Journal*, June) pp. 13—15.
Obelkevitch, James,
1976 *Religion in Rural Society: South Lindsay, 1825—1875*. Oxford, Oxford University Press.
O'Donovan, Oliver,
1984 *Begotten or Made?*. Oxford, Oxford University Press.
Pickering, W. S. F.,
1984 *Durkheim's Sociology of Religion*. London, Routledge and Kegan Paul.
Pike, Kenneth,
1962 *With Heart and Mind*. Grand Rapids, Eerdmans.
Poster, Mark,
1982 *Critical Theory of the Family*. London, Pluto.
Powell, David,
1975 *Anti-Religious Propaganda in the Soviet Union*. Cambridge, Ma, MIT Press.
Preston, Ronald,
1977 'Secularization and Renewal' (*Crucible*, April/June) pp. 68—77.
Ranson, Stewart, Bryman, Alan, and Hinings, Bob,
1977 *Clergy, Ministers and Priests*. London, Routledge and Kegan Paul.
Robertson, Roland,
1982 'Religion and Life', Paper read at International Sociological Association meeting in Mexico City, August.
1978 *Meaning and Change*. Oxford, Blackwell.

1970 *The Sociological Interpretation of Religion.* Oxford, Blackwell.

Rowell, Geoffrey,
1974 *Hell and the Victorians.* Oxford, Clarendon Press.

Rushton, P.,
1983 'Purification or Social Control? Ideologies of Reproduction and the Churching of Women after Childbirth', in E. Gamarnikow and others, eds., *The Public and the Private.* London, Heinemann.

Schaeffer, Francis,
1976 *How Should We Then Live?* Old Tappan, NJ, Fleming Revell.

Shallis, Michael,
1984 *The Silicon Idol.* Oxford, Oxford University Press.

Shiner, Larry,
1967 'The Concept of Secularization in Empirical Research' (*Journal for the Scientific Study of Religion*, 6) pp. 207–20.

Slater, Philip (ed.)
1976 *Religion and Culture in Canada.* Waterloo, Ontario, Wilfred Laurier University Press.

Smart, Ninian,
1973 *The Science of Religion and the Sociology of Knowledge.* Princeton, NJ, Princeton University Press.

Smith, Anthony,
1976 *Social Change.* London, Longman.

Spinks, Stephen,
1952 *Religion in Britain since 1900.* London, Andrew Dakers.

Stein, Maurice,
1960 *The Eclipse of Community.* Princeton, NJ, Princeton University Press.

Thomas, Keith,
1971 *Religion and the Decline of Magic.* London, Weidenfeld.

Towler, Robert, and Coxon, Anthony,
1979 *The Fate of the Anglican Clergy.* London, Macmillan.

Towler, Robert,
1974 *Homo religiosus: Sociological Problems in the Study of Religion.* London, Constable.

Turner, Bryan,
1983 *Religion and Social Theory.* London, Heinemann.

Troeltsch, Ernst,
1958 *Protestantism and Progress.* New York, Beacon Press.
1931 *The Social Teaching of the Christian Churches.* London, Allen and Unwin.

Tylor, E. B.,
1871 *Primitive Culture.* London, John Murray.

Vitz, Paul,
1977 *Psychology as Religion: the Cult of Self-Worship.* Tring, Lion Publishing.
Wallis, Roy,
1983 *The Elementary Forms of the New Religious Life.* London, Routledge and Kegan Paul.
Walter, J. A.,
1982 *The Human Home: the Myth of the Sacred Environment.* Tring, Lion Publishing.
1980 *A Long Way from Home.* Exeter, Paternoster, or *Sacred Cows.* Grand Rapids, Zondervan.
Weber, Max,
1976 *The Protestant Ethic and the Spirit of Capitalism.* New York, Scribners.
Weizenbaum, Joseph,
1984 *Computer Power and Human Reason.* Harmondsworth, Penguin.
Wickham, E. R.,
1957 *Church and People in an Industrial City.* London, Lutterworth.
Wilson, Bryan,
1982 *Religion in Sociological Perspective.* Oxford, Oxford University Press.
1982a 'The New Religions: Preliminary Considerations', in Eileen Barker, ed., 1982 q.v.
1976 *Contemporary Transformations of Religion.* Oxford, Oxford University Press.
1976b 'Some aspects of Secularization in The West' (*Japanese Journal of Religious Studies*, 3, 4, Dec.)
1973 *Magic and the Millennium: a Sociological Study of Religious Movements Among Tribal and Third World Peoples.* London, Heinemann.
1966 *Religion in a Secular Society.* Harmondsworth, Penguin.
Wuthnow, Robert, and others,
1984 *Cultural Analysis: the Work of Berger, Douglas, Foucault, and Habermas.* London, Routledge and Kegan Paul.
1982 'World Order and Religious Movements', in Eileen Barker, ed., 1982 q.v.
1976 'Recent Patterns of Secularization: a Problem of Generations?' (*American Sociological Review*, 41, 5) pp. 850–67.
Yinger, Milton,
1970 *The Scientific Study of Religion.* London, Collier-Macmillan.

Index